TAKE CARE

C. W. Brister

BROADMAN PRESS

Nashville, Tennessee

© Copyright 1978 • Broadman Press.

All rights reserved.

4255–78

ISBN: 0–8054–5578–7

Cover painting Print © 1965.

Dewey Decimal Classification: 248.4

Subject heading: CHRISTIAN LIFE//CHRISTIAN SOCIAL MINISTRIES

Library of Congress Catalog Card Number: 76–51022

Printed in the United States of America

To my mother, Elaine Holmes Brister, from whom I first learned the meaning of *care*
and
to my wife's parents, Floyd and Vergie Nugent, without whom life would have been so much less

Preface

Some years ago I wrote a little book entitled *People Who Care.* A dear friend, Gordon Clinard, saw a copy and jested, "When are you going to write the sequel about people who *don't* care?" Later, that gifted man was killed in a tragic automobile collision. I sometimes wonder if the world knows that it wasted such a splendid spirit.

At last, the sequel has been written. The words *take care* form both a caution and a command. How often we leave family members and friends with a parting admonition, "Take care!" It pleads for sanity in an insane world and tells a companion to proceed with caution in life. *Take care* is also signed to letters as a parting blessing among friends. It bids wise forethought in order to minimize risk along the way. There is a sense in which a person must care for himself in order to remain alive and to possess the ability to care for other persons.

We need to be careful. America has become a violent land of assault, robbery, rape, and murder. "It is enough to make us suspicious of everyone," a sensitive man observed. "No wonder city dwellers bolt their doors with multiple locking devices and sleep with watchdogs at their bedsides. I can understand why pickup trucks are armed with guns and why courses in self-defense are so popular." For reasons of personal safety and because of the high cost of caring in a brutal world, genuine brotherhood goes begging.

Paradoxically, *take care* is also a command to be obeyed. Christ's call to care echoes urgently across the centuries. He taught love for one's neighbor (Matt. 19:19; 22:39; Mark 12:31;

Gal. 5:14; Jas. 2:8) and for one's enemy as well (Matt. 5:44–46). Such concern springs from the fact that we have first been loved by the heavenly Father (1 John 4:19). Because of his compelling love and action through the cross, God's people are to love one another *and* the world for which Christ died (Matt. 28:19–20; 1 John 4:21).

I would agree with my late friend Clinard that there are many people who do not care. However, I am staking my faith and future on those who *do*. Caring, which orders our lives and sensitizes us to various needs of people, is a vanishing practice. True, countless acts of kindness are performed each day, but good news seldom makes the headlines. Kindness needs to be rekindled and wise compassion regained if we are to recover confidence in ourselves and risk life's venture as travelers together on planet earth.

Should you argue, "We live in a dog-eat-dog world where beating the competition is the name of the game," I would agree. Yet, I am deeply aware of other great realities like faith, hope, and love. The Bible promises that they alone will ultimately prevail (1 Cor. 13:13). Eyes of faith see a kinder, softer world in the making. The process of ethical sensitivity, appreciation of personal worth, family loyalty, and genuine concern for one's neighbor has already begun.

This book is your personal invitation to become a part of tomorrow's caring people. It addresses Christian laypersons and professionals who engage daily in caring conversations. Helping is examined in the context of biblical faith. It is viewed, not optionally, but as a given aspect of God's agenda for the church. The first four chapters address the *being* aspect of caregiving; they characterize people who care. Each of the remaining chapters addresses a particular aspect of *doing* ministry: caring skills, friendship, family needs, crisis counseling, older people, illness, death, and grief.

Fittingly, examples from helping situations are provided as models. The names, locations, and circumstances of persons mentioned in case histories have all been changed. Conversations are the substance of what people said, rather than their actual words. Chapters 5 and 10 parallel similar discussions in *People Who Care,* though they have been revised. All Scripture quotations are from the Revised Standard Version, unless otherwise indicated.

Warmest thanks to my friends Carolyn Weatherford and the late Glendon McCollough, colleague David Fite, son Mark A. Brister, and wife, Gloria, each of whom read the manuscript and offered suggestions which I have taken seriously. My secretary, Cindy Gail Bryant, carefully typed the final version of the manuscript. Life is infinitely richer because of their care and companionship.

C. W. Brister

Contents

1 Who Cares?

Two Christian friends were lunching in a restaurant popular among business and professional persons. They had talked of God's gracious providence in their lives and of the disparity between *have* and *have-not* persons everywhere. While counting their blessings, both men recognized, with true pathos, that many of earth's citizens were less fortunate than themselves. One mentioned a mutual friend's wife, stricken with cancer; also, a physician who had died following a stroke. Some distressing international news was noted.

"You know," said Bill, "a person has to be an incurable optimist every day, or he would soon give up. It's a wonder there aren't more suicides in this country than there are."

An interesting turn in their conversation came as they identified people facing concerns and crises: the young who fear that they are inadequate for life's challenge, the old who worry about being forgotten, and the poor who resent their apparently inescapable dependency. "They need help," Bert ventured, "yet many people do not seem to care."

The observation prompted Bill, the host, to mention a mutual acquaintance—a driven man, whose life-style had become defensive, self-preserving, falsified, and vindictive. "Why does Jim Vinning put people down in every situation," he queried, "when what they need is encouragement and validation?" He cited a recent instance in which an esteemed colleague had suffered abuse at Vinning's hands.

"Perhaps it's because he never received a blessing from his own father," replied his observant guest. "People have a hard time prizing others if they have seldom felt esteem for

11

themselves." "Maybe he belittles people because he received a lot of abuse, not love, while growing up," Bill replied.

A profound question resides at the core of that noonday conversation: Who cares—for individuals and families facing stress, for institutions and social systems under pressure—in contemporary culture? We appear to live in a land of violence and vindictiveness, of nomads and strangers, of personal intimidation and social injustice. It is not merely the helpless minority, ethnics, aged, and poor who face greed, competition, indifference, and deceit. Many white, middle-class citizens, at the peak of prosperity and productivity, suffer a profound uneasiness, a sense of dislocation, and a feeling of abandonment. Self-confidence has been eroded by constant competitiveness, financial instability, changing social landmarks, technological evolution, failing health, and the struggle to survive. Much distress and suffering are incurred in trying to live out choices which other people or events have made for us.

People who care, meanwhile, are a vanishing breed. Many folk claim to care: agents of conglomerate corporations seeking increased profits, real estate brokers building fortunes off speculative property transactions, builders permitting flawed construction and planned obsolescence, healers performing endless rites on patients, and parents who claim to cherish, yet neglect and abuse, their children. The list of care-pretenders is endless, while genuine care-givers are scarce. There are luminous exceptions to this looking-out-for-number-one attitude. Ministering persons, basically supportive of the best in our human venture, must be encouraged and freed to care.

Care as Promise and as Problem

The tension between avarice and altruism, selfishness and service, egotism and compassion is not a new struggle. Biblical faith has called mankind to care from the beginning. Indeed, the whole message of divine mercy hinges on confidence in a caring God. "I have loved you with an everlasting love; therefore I have continued my faithfulness to you," (Jer. 31:3) God promised the ancient Israelites, exiled in Babylon. The twin themes of God's generous creation and gracious redemption are major chords in his providential composition. They are blended in contrast with his righteousness, justice, and condemnation of sin (Rom. 5:8-21). Because the Father supplies all our needs "according to his riches in glory in Christ Jesus" (Phil. 4:19), we, in turn, are to "abound" with generosity toward others (2 Cor. 8:7-15).[1] That is God's universal call to care.

In what follows, *care* will be used to mean *helpful response to humanity's hurt and search for wholeness.* It is a classic biblical term, noteable when absent in human experience, as when the psalmist cried: "No man cared for my soul" (Ps. 142:4 KJV). Jesus Christ used *care* precisely as supportive action in behalf of another individual in the good Samaritan story. The helpful traveler spotted a wounded man by the roadside, "went to him and bound up his wounds . . . , brought him to an inn, and took care of him." He paid the innkeeper, saying: "Take care of him; and whatever more you spend, I will repay you when I come back" (Luke 10:34-35). The Bible traces God's vulnerability to human pain through the life, death, and resurrection of Jesus Christ. Because he cared, God's persons are to care by *doing* the truth (Jas. 2:14-18). Love takes action; it is more than sentiment. One who cares will "lay down his life" in the human venture (John 15:13). We acknowledge, then, that caring is costly behavior.

Care will also be used in a *symbolic* sense, as the Bible itself uses it, to express attitudes of concern and compassion which motivate ministry. This is the *being* aspect of religious experience which precedes doing or expressing faith. The timeless words of Jesus to Nicodemus illustrate how care, in biblical usage, conveys both symbolic and literal intent: "God so loved the world that he gave his only Son, that whoever believes in him should not perish but have eternal life" (John 3:16). The heavenly Father's saving deeds sprang from his great heart of love. It will be helpful to recognize that care, also in contemporary usage, moves back and forth between motivation (being) and action (doing). Words like *care, concern, compassion, regard, attentiveness,* and *solicitude* will be used interchangably with *love.* If they appear ambiguous, it is simply because they possess symbol-laden dimensions of meaning which cannot be separated from each other.

Christian care-giving presupposes a context of risky investment and of involvement in bold mission ventures because life matters. Care is the fundamental capacity to cherish a person, family, group, idea, program, or cause to the degree that one acts willingly in the object's behalf. Care both sensitizes one to need and spends itself in behalf of persons, causes, ideas, or structures affecting life. Helping is the driving force at the center of Christian character. It's presence or absence is a clue to one's self-structure—a life-style of egocentricity or generosity. Care is not merely a religious duty; it is a human obligation in the community of man.

One does not, then, have to be a Christian to want to help. The Jews, who possess much of our biblical wisdom and acknowledge a special God-relationship, have a splendid record of helping anguished people everywhere. Citizens in developing nations, landless through much of their history, are drawn to the world's dispossessed with splendid generosity. Much of mankind's medical progress, knowledge of how to help, and actual care of sufferers has been the work of people who did not acknowledge Jesus Christ as their Savior. Participants in the so-called helping professions, like psychiatry and social work, may look not to God but to humanistic sources of wisdom as a basis for caring. It becomes clear from a study of church history that Christians have sometimes been, to their shame, far less considerate of human needs than other people.

On the other hand, sainthood has been so intertwined with the notion of self-sacrifice that Christians may be tempted to put other people's good before their own. Such perverted altruism, carried to an extreme, makes one a doormat for the world's feet but not a wise helper to treat its wounds. The

Bible speaks of loving God and others in a manner similar to the way in which one has been loved and loves oneself (1 John 4:19; Deut. 6:5; Matt. 22:36-40). Extreme, pathological self-denial can lead to constant, if not always conscious, frustration and resentment. Care, wisely given, is both God's eternal promise of steadfast love and man's positive response in faithful service. Paradoxically, the context for such compassionate living may be constrictive or constructive.

Caring in a World of Systems

Concern takes many forms, from respect for institutional work rules and laws that protect life to physical culture and health maintenance; from a missionary's mobile clinic in some primitive land to an attorney's assisting a widow in a major estate settlement; from prayer for God's persons everywhere to visiting a patient in a hospital. It may involve a single conversation or extensive family counseling.

Such expressions remind us that Christianity has both personal and group dimensions. Our life in Christ is like the two sides of a coin. On the one side lies our individual identity, on the other our group identity. The apostle Paul likened the church to a "body" with many interdependent parts (1 Cor. 12:14-27; Eph. 4:11-12; Col. 1:18). One's faith is intensely personal, a fact reinforced in our individualistic society. Each aspect of Christ's body is unique and essential. Yet, gifts like eyes, hands, and feet do not exist in isolation. They intereact as parts of a living system.

We are born into a genetic family, take its name, develop its ideals, and express its characteristics in unfolding behavior. Just so, we are born into God's family, with a unique faith heritage and denominational expression, and live out a group identity. Neither families nor church groups, however, live in isolation from culture. In earlier days, one's identity was linked to basic groups like family, church, and school, to the land one tilled for survival, and to personal encounters with one's fellow citizens. Today, one-fifth of all Americans move on the average of once each year. We live in vast urban sprawls, lost in anonymous crowds, among a nation of strangers. Masses of individuals, attracted to the city's jobs, resources, options, and services, experience an identity crisis. The French sociologist Emile Durkheim called this phenomenon *anomie*—persons who are "without a name." Familiar landmarks are lost. Gaining a sense of selfhood, surviving new perils, and mustering courage to care become more difficult. The familiar means of gaining identity, fostering survival, and prizing others seem to have evaporated.

Scholars have sought to interpret the varied influences and factors which shape our lives in terms of systems theory.[2] We may speak of a person as a total system, having unique physiological *subsystems* (heart, nerves, muscles, and so on), living in an ecological system. Our attitudes, values, and behavior result from complex forces operating as a unified whole. The body's secondary systems depend upon, interact with, and, if unhealthy, can endanger one's total life system. Think for a moment of some basic systems that influence our behavior.

The ecological system into which an individual is born— race, nationality, geographical location, social class, neighborhood, weather, and so on;

The biological system with which one is equipped—sex, body size, intelligence, eye and hair color, birth defects, and the like;

The family system—may be open, trustful, loving, affirming, freeing family members for life; may be closed, suspicious, demanding, rejecting, and psychologically destructive; or a combination of such factors in a midrange of relationships;

The community, social, economic, governmental, and educational systems affect preparation for life, its privileges, limits, tasks, and opportunities for a meaningful existence;

The religious system casts one toward a fundamentalistic,

liberal, agnostic, reactionary, or healthy life-style. It also determines one's group affiliation: Jewish, Buddhist, Mormon, Christian, and so on.

Imagine having to function on any given day influenced by subsystems' effects like being overweight, going to work with a migraine headache, having a minor accident on the freeway, preferring to be at home in bed, having to shop for groceries before stores close, and preparing dinner for oneself and one's spouse. We can guess what might happen if there is a change in even one subsystem: maybe nothing; perhaps something major. The effects would depend upon many reciprocal factors, actions, and reactions.

I mention such systems because we are not entirely free to pursue exclusive, personal objectives in the modern world. What happens in Tokyo, Cairo, Jerusalem, Moscow, Hong Kong, New Delhi, and Buenos Aires affects us. Other people's needs touch our lives, and paradoxically what we do affects other persons. Thus caring occurs in a world of systems. Because of secularized care sources like the United Way, Red Cross, and CARE, we feel removed from persons needing help. We do not even know about most people's anguished struggles for survival. Or, we assume that "George is doing it"—some do-gooder is out there making care possible.

Caring is as personal as a mother's touch upon her growing child; yet, it also involves corporate effort. A system, like the Cooperative Program of giving in Baptist life, takes one individual's contribution, plus the gifts of persons in many congregations, and unites them in support of ministries throughout the world. Such acts of helpfulness are quite intentional, though, from an outsider's perspective, they might appear spontaneous. Like an army, care depends upon the working both of a shared multitude and a sensitive minority of helpers.

In an era of coalitions, task forces, and mass movements one writer called the individual carer "a pathetic figure in our time." There is just one thing wrong with such logic. It isn't true! No helping action, community agency, or global resource is available until someone cares. Care, the wellspring of all the actions this book proposes, is rooted in personal response to God and respect for human personality. That care must be corporate to count is equally true. Care's purpose is redemptive. Its place is any center of existence which holds the possibility of life, meaning, and spiritual wholeness. Its people are professionals and amateurs alike who claim to be God's people.

The Church As People Who Care

Thus far, we have viewed care as a clue to one's self-structure and as a source of satisfaction in serviceable living. We have noted God's eternal promise to care for his creation and its fulfillment in Christian history. We have seen how care moves from the *being* to the *doing* stage of life, amid mixed motives and complex systems. In this foundational discussion, it remains to acknowledge that Christ created the church as people who care. This suggests an important principle: *We must discover God's purpose for the church in each new generation.*[3] Each congregation and denomination should inquire of the Lord what his will and purpose are for this new day and age. It is from him that we gain wisdom and courage to live.

Writers of the New Testament—apostles, pastors, and teachers of the first century—did not think in our terms about the church. Little detailed, explicit information about the church's nature, life, and work can be determined authoritatively from the Scriptures.

Interestingly, only one of the four Gospel writers recalled that Jesus used the term *church,* and he recorded its use on only two occasions. In Matthew 16:18, the concept is wholly spiritual and its origin attributed to Christ's initiative and man's response. The second instance, Matthew 18:17, refers to church discipline and implies, without any explanation, a brotherhood having social and organizational aspects. While our Lord perceived the church in a specific, local sense, there was implied a universal quality as well. The other Gospels assume the spiritual reality that constitutes the church without using the term *church* or defining any equivalent term. Still, we have guidelines for charting the church's purpose.

1. Jesus Christ created the church initially by calling individual persons to faith in himself.

When the Pharisees criticized him for talking with sinners, Jesus explained his purpose: "I came that they may have life, and have it abundantly" (John 10:10). The Bible takes for granted that life, physical and spiritual, originates with God and that his Son makes this life explicit (Gen. 1:27-31; John 1:1-13).

The New Testament term *ekklesia*, translated "church," implies God's true congregation—persons called from sin and darkness into salvation and light. Those who believed the Word whom God sent, Jesus of Nazareth, became his followers—soldiers under his command. This is why the Jews accused him of sedition against Rome. Whereas the Roman soldier swore allegiance to his emperor, Jesus' disciples took an oath of loyalty to him alone (Acts 5:29).

Various terms are used in the Scriptures to describe the church's nature. Their rich symbolism and implications can help us identify the work that a church should do. Early Christians were nicknamed the followers of *the One* by outsiders or pagans. He was their *Kyrios*, or commander, their leader, model, and Lord—as well as Savior. They were not Caesar's but Christ's: the people of God, a colony of heaven, the temple of the Holy Spirit, a royal priesthood, a holy nation, God's building, the body of Christ.

Paradoxically, the church is both the universal (mystical) body of Christ and local congregations of believers.

2. The church's first task is faithfulness to Christ her Lord.

There is only one ministry, and we are permitted to participate in it as God's partners. The apostle Paul said that this ministry belonged to Jesus, first, then to his church. "God was in Christ reconciling the world to himself . . . and entrusting to us the message of reconciliation. So we are ambassadors for Christ, God making his appeal through us" (2 Cor. 5:19-20). Christians are ministers of the gospel of redemption.

This ministry is not something which belongs to one group (the ordained) within the church. God allows all his people to share in it. We are "workers together" with him to bring salvation to the world. Also, Christians should demonstrate a way of life which is valid for persons and nations.

3. We may identify the church's ministry, and our own, by recalling key incidents in Jesus' ministry.

First, what was the passion that prompted Jesus to leave his heavenly Father's house and to identify with citizens of earth? He refused the fame and fortune of an earthly empire (Luke 4:1-13). Human praise and approval, or criticism and hostility, did not throw him off course. In Matthew 23:37 he is seen weeping over the spiritual burdens and physical needs of ancient Jerusalem's multitudes. Fortunately our Lord did more than cry. He identified with men held in the grip of moral chaos and a religion of fear. "He had compassion for them, because they were harassed and helpless, like sheep without a shepherd" (Matt. 9:36). Love carried him to Calvary that he might give eternal life to all who would believe in his name (John 3:16).

Second, we find Jesus' concept of his ministry, and therefore of ours, expressed on a return visit to his hometown synagogue.

And he came to Nazareth, where he had been brought up; and he went to the synagogue, as his custom was, on the sabbath day. And he stood up to read; and there was given to him the book of the prophet Isaiah. He opened the book and found the place where it was written, "The Spirit of the Lord is upon me, because he has anointed me [here is the ministry] to preach good news to the poor. He has sent me to proclaim release to the captives and recovering of sight to the blind, to set at liberty those who are oppressed, to proclaim the acceptable year of the Lord." And he closed the book, and gave it back to the attendant, and sat down; and the eyes of all in the synagogue were fixed on him. And he began to say to them, "Today this scripture has been fulfilled in your hearing" (Luke 4:16-21).

His words, based upon Isaiah 61:1-2, found acceptance and approval among the hearers. They spoke well of him as "Joseph's son," a hometown boy who had made good.

The climate of their conversation changed considerably, however, when Jesus recalled Old Testament instances when God's gracious action included non-Jews: (1) Elijah sent to the widow of Zarephath in the land of Sidon, and (2) Elisha's cleansing a Syrian leper, Naaman, a nonbeliever. "When they heard this, all in the synagogue were filled with wrath. And they rose up and put him out of the city, and led him to the brow of the hill on which their city was built, that they might throw him down headlong. But passing through the midst of them he went away" (Luke 4:28-30).

Why were they prompted to chase Jesus out of town and to pitch him off a cliff? Jesus annoyed the Jewish covenant community because he insisted that God's love is universal. It includes the sinners, poor, handicapped, captives, and oppressed persons everywhere. Furthermore, he failed to work through approved channels of the Jewish hierarchy with the chief priests and elders. Refusing to discriminate or conform to their prejudices, Jesus called all kinds of people to do his work.

The Messiah of God proclaimed a new covenant of salvation that was sealed in his suffering love upon the cross. We learn from him that service to persons must cross all human barriers of race, culture, politics, and social standing. The gospel is at home in every situation of human need. Churches today must find ways to remove or transcend barriers that separate their members from other persons and groups. Christ's lordship must be extended to all the world—science, art, government, commerce, and leisure—where personality is blighted by sin and suffering. This requires skill and mutually planned action.

4. The church's tasks are basic continuing activities under-taken in obedience to Christ's command and example.

The church may be viewed as a fellowship of ultimate concerns. It is not some celestial body of invisible saints. Rather, it is a spiritual brotherhood of persons who are committed to Christ and the advancement of his kingdom. Thus the Christian's ultimate loyalty is to Christ—the one true head of the church.

The basic biblical word for the local fellowship of Christ's followers is *koinōnia*—implying a ministering congregation. They are people who care. By its very nature the Christian *koinōnia* involves a shared ministry by all the *laos*—the people of God. This includes pastors and people alike. Thus the church is an organism, Christ's body, requiring identification through baptism and obedience in discipleship. It is under orders (Matt. 28:19-20) to change the world. In every age and culture this living system expresses its life through organized forms or churches.

What is the church for? Primarily, the congregation lives for God's sake in worship, for the world's sake in proclamation and witness, and for its own sake in nurture and ministry. It has lived out the kingdom of God in specific communities across the world in every period of history. The church's mission of evangelism and ministry forms the basis of discussion in the remaining chapters of this book.

At the outset we should affirm that Christian living "worthy of the gospel" requires the presence and guidance of the Holy Spirit. The new humanity about which the apostles wrote is the fellowship of God's Spirit (2 Cor. 3:17). We rely upon his power to interpret the mind of Christ, to convict consciences and cleanse from sin, and to guide members of congregations in ways of righteousness. God's Spirit makes the church's task possible and worthwhile (John 14:16–17; Acts 1:4-5,8). He is the One who sensitizes us for mission and sets us free to care.

2 Gaining the Freedom to Care

It was Easter Sunday. The pastor of a black congregation had issued a challenge to his people to "rise up and build" a new worship center. The present location had served a past generation, he noted convincingly, but a new day called for improved facilities. Black congregants often respond in dialogue with their worship leaders, offering arousing amens of encouragement. An elderly man verbally supported his pastor's proposal when suddenly he was attacked by a young man in the congregation. He was beaten with a club.

Friends rushed the aged churchman to a local hospital. It was the most helpful thing they knew to do. His son, however, vowed to avenge the attack, went home, got a handgun, and drove to the agitator's residence. The son was shot and killed by his father's attacker, in an unexpected turn of events.

"What a stupid way to care," one might surmise. "Why try to vindicate an aging parent's advocacy of progress with a gun? Why get oneself killed under the guise of helpfulness?" The incident provides an example of many people's inability, unwillingness, confusion about, and lack of freedom to care. Part of this inability is due to ignorance about caring skills; part to spiritual and psychic bondages which hinder helping; part to some victims who want no help; part to motives that are suspect; and part to times which are "out of joint."

This Easter incident seems farfetched until we reflect upon the unwise ways individuals, families, groups, even nations have attempted to care—for themselves and others.

Here is a carpenter who has been diagnosed as having a serious skin cancer. Rather than returning to the physician

23

for essential surgery and radiation therapy, he purchased a potent paste mixed by a herbalist. A "friend" had told him about the herb doctor's success with cases similar to his own. He used the herbal substance daily but declined in health. In a matter of months he died, almost as though by suicide. His distraught family was left penniless.

I have visited parts of the world which, in centuries past, were subjected to the Spanish Inquisition. Under the pretense of keeping the Roman Catholic Church holy and its doctrines pure, thousands of persons were tried by ecclesiastical courts. Severe questioning was pursued under the guise of orthodoxy. Investigations were conducted without regard for human rights. Torture chambers were constructed in cathedral basements and, in heaven's name, screaming communicants were placed in cages like wild beasts, stretched on racks like animal skins, and bent double in inhuman pain. The previous facts stand as ghastly reminders of what idolatrous religion can do.

In America, striking workers have closed businesses which have supported a region financially for generations. Thoughtless plant owners, on the other hand, have paid minimum wages to impoverished workers in the name of generosity. I have lived in the rural South where absentee landlords kept sharecroppers in dependency and poverty, not unlike the pre-Civil War era. I have also lived in cities, like New York, where angry citizens, in the name of concern, have burned entire blocks of buildings and turned playgrounds into battlefields. Wars have been fought in our homeland, the Western hemisphere, and across the earth in the name of "making the world safe for democracy." Assassinations have been attempted, governments toppled, and financial empires destroyed in the name of helpfulness.

All Are Not Free to Care

Gaining the freedom to care requires group values distinguished by a conviction that life counts, a sense of justice, and the establishment of dignity and integrity in life. An individual ethic is also essential: self-worth, sensitivity to suffering, and a stance of compassion toward persons in need. Care-givers are purpose people who thrust themselves into life for its betterment. This is the morality of care. Like Moses of old, such helpers have discovered that "the place on which [they] are standing is holy ground" (Ex. 3:5). As they examine it, see what it has to reveal, detect its shape, they understand its holiness in terms of God's presence and redemptive action.

Someone has said that experience is not an experience until you have experienced it. So it is with caring. Needs for helping lie all around us. Usually, in some crucial incident, decision, stage of life, or casualty, we discover whether we really care.

I once visited with a beautiful young woman who had discovered that she was a misfit in the field of social work. The daughter of a minister, she married a devoted lay leader in her church. Gay Sims had majored in sociology in college but, within five years, had moved through two career fields in an effort to "gain freedom to care." "I discovered that I did not have the compassion to work with hurting people," said Gay. "It's best for me not to be in touch with them. I just couldn't take it."

Her excuse for escaping the crunch of humanity's hurt might be tagged rationalization. Mechanisms of defense, said Sigmund Freud, are brought to our rescue at both conscious and unconscious levels. Gay may have been thin-skinned; other people's problems may have become her own under pressure. She may have had a fragile self-system or a doubtful sense of her own worth as God's person. Social work for one uncertain about her own identity is like walking on eggshells. Gay discovered that some underprivileged persons function with a value system—about sex, money, and violence—that seemed almost subhuman (at least unchristian). She experienced the language of the poor as foreign and their outrage with life as threatening to her own safety and sanity.

Such a response of inadequacy feelings is understandable.

It certainly does not mean that she had no compassion for people and never took a stance of care. Once she had *experienced it*, she discovered an unfreeness to help certain individuals. Her inadequacy in one area, however, did not deter her from a serviceable life. It actually freed her to care on a new and wiser plane.

Ineptness stops some persons short of embracing the world's wounded citizens; fear hinders others. A private plane crashed in a Midwestern state close to a major highway. The pilot seemed to point his tiny craft at the four-lane strip of interstate road in an effort to effect a safe landing. A man and his eight-year-old daughter were discovered in the fiery ruins by a bus driver. The driver halted his bus at the crash site, hurried to pull surviving victims from the craft, and called to passengers for help. Instead, they screamed: "That thing is going to blow up! Get back! The gas tank may explode! Don't go near it!" Several of the bystanders innocently got out their cameras and began taking photographs of the crash scene.

Finally, in a desperate effort to save lives, the bus driver pled for someone to assist him in carrying the badly wounded pilot to safety. One man from all the crowd stepped forward to help. Fear about their own personal safety froze some observers in apparent indifference. Others registered a kind of bewilderment about what was happening. They seemed stuck in a state of shock. Later, a man said: "I still care about people, but it would be much easier not to care." That spirit sums up the way life is for a lot of people right now. They don't want to get involved.

Somewhere on the spectrum between ineptness, on the one hand, and indifference on the other lie added reasons why people don't care.

Annie Dillard, in her poetical reflections as a *Pilgrim at Tinker Creek*, quotes a Virginia neighbor: "Seem like we're just set down here and don't nobody know why."[1] Thoughtful members of the human community revisit often the deepest questions that existence raises for them. Pondering *why* we are "set down here" leads eventually to faith or despair, to meaningful concern or maddening chaos.

Ignorance, like that of the Virginia mountain woman, may be bliss for some. Still, what we do not know can hurt us and others. A missionary appointed to minister overseas experienced the limits of serviceability as a hospital chaplain. He discovered his ignorance about most hospital techniques being experienced by both patients and the medical staff. Beyond barriers of language and culture, he felt an enormous separation lodged in each patient's pain and his woeful lack of information. In an effort to correct his "don't nobody know why" plight, the missionary sought paramedic skills. He wanted to touch pained bodies with care, not merely to comfort wounded spirits with words alone.

People who are looking out for number one in mad pursuit of power, prestige, and pleasure view humanitarianism as stupid. Greed is their god; they seek prominence, not places of service. I remember as a youth trying to persuade a wealthy businessman to purchase advertising space in our high school newspaper. As we talked in his office one day our attention turned to things that matter. I spoke idealistically of my devotion to Christ who "went about doing good" (Acts 10:38). His squelching reply fell with a crunch: "Do-gooders don't amount to much!" Later, I learned that he owned more than one hundred rental houses in my home city's black ghetto. They went unpainted and unattended, save for his monthly rent collections, for years. His greed oppressed many people.

Has not this attitude of "get it while you can," regardless of the long-term effects, led to environmental distress, economic imbalances, and strife between the world's *haves* and *have nots?* It isn't that we have not cared but that we prized our own welfare above all else. Now, like the greedy rich man in Christ's parable, America's "soul is [being] required" as a repayment to the Creator (Luke 12:18–21).

Paradoxically, it was the spirit of rugged individualism,

vision, patience, and prudent effort that characterized the early pioneer environment of America. Ours was a land of inexhaustable resources—an endless frontier—to be explored and exploited in isolation from other countries Industrial production, an expanding economy, new markets in other parts of the world, and the rise of multinational corporate structures excited investors. One of the by-products of this environment was a bureaucratic approach to life. Now we have moved into a time of shortages of energy and natural resources, pollution and recycled products, and depersonalization where technology is king. We have discovered that we must live in the world we've fashioned. To improve it we must care for the earth and its inhabitants, its Creator, and his basic purposes in creation.

Freedom Through Awareness

When change occurs, confidence in old ways which proved too costly or unwise gives way to faith in the new—in things more worthy of faith. Caring is a life-style whose time has come (once again). Man has been tricked into trusting the wrong things. Money as the summum bonum (the supreme good from which all others are derived) fails its pursuer. International monetary policies, the fluctuating price of gold, the inflation rate, wage-price spirals, energy resource limits, and increased levels of taxation make money more of a problem than a solution. Excursions into war highlight the limits of bombs and guns and illuminate the power of nationalistic pride and self-determination. Alcohol, drugs—whether by prescription in middle-class respectability or by pushers in underworld illegality—sex, physical culture, and cosmetic surgery are avoidance techniques, not ways of truly coping with life.

Some individuals have tried it all: retreating into past nostalgia, dropping out of the present, joining the extremists (who, on the far right resist change and the far left coerce change), and anticipating some sort of millennial holocaust. Many reactionary religious leaders advocate either simplistic solutions or legalistic formulas for survival—ideas which ultimately constrict one's own self, family, and society. Also, positive thinking cults, with both secular and religious advocates, prescribe a positive mental attitude as the key to success. Each of these stances is an effort to gain strength over stress and to simplify existence.

The modern mystic Walter Starcke has said: "I have spent many years with a feeling that I was not in my right place and right time. I got along in the world, but I never felt quite at home. Now I realize that I was in my right place and in my right time, only the right time for the main purpose of my life just hadn't come yet."[2] Starcke discovered that his main job in life was not tearing down but building up. He holds that some of our finest opportunities for service come not during, but at the end of a revolutionary era. He calls this sharing in "the ultimate revolution," through a morality of grace.

Gaining the freedom to care comes first through bondage assessment—discovering why people don't care. Freedom is also gained through achieving awareness of what has failed and what has worked. Awareness also implies sensitivity and sensible approaches for helping. America's recent history of varied liberation movements, for example, illustrated the need to care with wisdom and justice for *all* persons.

It is said that Harlem's blacks a generation ago shared a common condition but not a common consciousness. Their pain was internalized for years until black poets, turned prophets, divided flesh from bone and called millions of black persons to a new destiny. Their frenzied concern, with fire in the streets and determination to "get whitey," was produced more by rage than by love. This is verified in ethnic studies, like *Black Rage,* by psychiatrists William H. Grier and Price M. Cobbs. They explored the depths of black self-hatred, then pushed their brothers to develop basic human values—to find an identity, a sense of worth, to relate to others, to love, work, and create. There is great truth in the appeal for nonviolence by Martin Luther King, Jr., who advocated *Strength to Love.* Our world's hope, not that of blacks' alone, is that love will prevail.

The struggle by minorities for dignity, justice, and equal opportunity in life is illustrative of the human condition. We must each come to feel blessed in order to possess what Myron Madden has termed "the power to bless." God's love can startle us into awareness of "the others" and shape our gifts to meet actual needs. Any benefit my neighbor receives from me, paradoxically, comes from my prior loyalties to God and myself (Matt. 22:36–40). As one obeys the dictum, "To thine own self be true," he gathers inner resources to become "a friend to any man."

Freedom Through Healthy Motives

God's persons are supposed to "love one another" as a fundamental clue to Christian character (John 15:12). More, they are to love the world for which Christ died and bring its citizens to faith in the Father. Biblical writers addressed believers as people on mission: "You are a chosen race, a royal priesthood, a holy nation, God's own people, that you may declare the wonderful deeds of him who called you out of darkness into his marvelous light" (1 Pet. 2:9). Declaring God's love to wrongdoers and righteous persons alike requires not only sensitivity but also inner strength and secure motives.

Why does someone want to help another "in Christ's stead?" There are many possible answers. [3]

The Bible commands us to "love your neighbor as yourself" (Mark 12:31); to "do justice and to love kindness" (Micah 6:8); even to "love your enemies" (Matt. 5:44). Since the Bible is God's Word, we try to obey it and seek forgiveness when we fail.

Jesus himself is our model of true humanity, spiritual wholeness, mature devotion, and careful discipline.[4] God's Son gave us an example that we "should follow in his steps" (1 Pet. 2:21). He spent a great deal of time and energy in ministering to others, healing the sick, and making the blind to see.

Those who claim Christ as Lord want to be as much like him as is humanly possible.

Jesus taught us that service rendered to "one of the least of these my brethren" would be accounted as service to himself (Matt. 25:40). Some people hearing those words become benefactors, not because they prize their fellow human beings but in order to obtain a heavenly reward. Possibly, people have founded hospitals, libraries, or schools, not to redistribute the world's wealth or to relieve suffering and ignorance, but to buy what is sometimes called "fire insurance." You may know someone, for example, who lived a somewhat godless life, then, almost as an afterthought, attempted to put themselves right with God. The desire for reward parallels closely the wish to atone for past sins, to "make it up" to society for what one did or failed to do. In the Matthew 25:31–46 account, concerning the last judgment, the helpers were actually surprised with the Father's blessing.

We know of well-intentioned people who tie strings to their generosity because they wish, perhaps unconsciously, to manipulate another person. Many would-be helpers are controlling, bossy people. One man said of his domineering mother: "She manipulated me with a golden glove." Eventually, following a complete nervous collapse and breakthrough via psychotherapy, he gained inner freedom to grow.

Some people care because they crave, again perhaps unconsciously, human approval. They wish to be liked or to gain prestige in the eyes of people, so they render favors, pull strings, and open doors of opportunity for those about them.

We have noted multifaceted motives for helping—obeying scriptural commands, following Christ's model, hoping for heavenly rewards, easing one's conscience, desiring to control other people's lives, and needing social approval. A more subtle motive is the helper's need to feel superior to certain helpees. Contributors to Goodwill Industries, for example—where moderately handicapped persons work to restore clothing, furniture, and household articles for use and sale—may have the smug feeling of being unlike "those poor creatures." One may feel superior in at least two ways: sentimental about life's victims and smart about tax breaks accruing to donors of usable merchandise.

The Bible warns us not to become "judges and dividers" of our fellowmen (Luke 12:13–15). Judging human motivations is God's work, not man's. We see external circumstances. God looks upon the heart and discerns one's true intentions (Heb. 4:12–13). Care-giving is so complex, however, that a helper needs intuitive wisdom in understanding his own motives. Since "each of us shall give account of himself to God," we should recognize the psychic motors that drive our lives (Rom.14:12).

John, the apostle, helped us answer the question, What makes Christian care unique? He viewed helping, by individuals and congregations, as grateful response to what God has done for us. "We love, because he first loved us," marks gratitude to God as "the bottom line" for ministry (1 John 4:19). Love takes the initiative, risks dangers, sees new possibilities—through intentional and spontaneous expressions—in order to help persons and change structures which harm life. Above all, Christian persons reach out in mission and ministry because Jesus Christ has called us to care. That is the church's redemptive task.

3 A Time to Care

One Independence Day a newspaper editor noted all the things that were right and dependable in the United States.

The food is on the table.
The paycheck keeps coming in.
The business door is open.
The children are at play.
The school bell keeps ringing.
The church door is open.
The police are chasing crooks.
The United States mint is printing money.
The courts are ruling.
The Air Force is flying.
The Social Security check is arriving.
The Congress is debating.
The politician is campaigning.
The mail is being delivered.
The newspapers are publishing.
The flags keep flying.
The telephones are ringing.
The cars are moving.
The family survives stress.
The holidays are being celebrated.

"No Pollyanna condition exists," noted the writer. "All is not completely well. But on this day—July 4—some things, some mighty important things, are right in our homeland." America moves right on—through times of war and peace, internal anarchy and harmony—because hardworking people care. We need not wait for a time of personal crisis, social conflict, or global disruption to feel concern. A sense of timing is crucial, however, when needs do arise. Consider the following example.

Friends of a wealthy oilman and his wife were shocked when an official verdict of homicide-suicide was made concerning their deaths by the county medical examiner. The couple had everything! He was an internationally known sportsman and philanthropist. The middle-aged pair lived in a fortress-style mansion, complete with security guards, gardener, maid, cook, and chauffeur. They were the envy of their city's social set but they were in deep need. No one suspected it. The two were found dead one weekend: he with .38 caliber pistol wounds in the head, neck, and shoulder; she with a fatal wound in the abdomen.

We can only imagine the malady which struck and eroded their marriage: cooling of affections, chronic absenteeism, self-centeredness, sexual involvement with a third party, ill health, alcohol or drug abuse, or pointless arguments and fighting. The price of lovelessness was paid in full. He at fifty-five, she at fifty, had so much of life ahead of them. What if someone—a minister, family member, or friend—could have detected that they were traveling separate paths? Perhaps one conversation could have challenged their life directions or cautioned them to share or called them to fresh devotion. Time ran out. There were no hours left to care.

What is most personal is most universal. Probing this story reminds us of our need to be fully present with other persons. It signifies the perils of preoccupation with one's own things, of procrastination concerning explosive issues, of deafness to someone's call for help. Jesus, in his day, challenged insensitivity to great opportunity. "To what then shall I compare the men of this generation, and what are they like?" (Luke 7:31), he inquired. He compared the Pharisees and scribes to children sitting in the marketplace, who called to one another: "We piped to you, and you did not dance; we wailed, and you did not weep." He reminded them that when John the Baptist

came, eating no bread and drinking no wine, they said he
had a demon. Then, when the Son of man came eating and
drinking, they called him "a glutton and a drunkard, a friend
of tax collectors and sinners!" Jesus concluded that God's wisdom is shown to be true by all who accept it (Luke 7:31–
34). The point of his analogy? Uncaring criticism reveals spiritual insensibility and hardness of heart.

How easy it is for us to sit back and find fault with folk
when things aren't going our way. We often belittle our belea-
guered comrades when they are beset by temptations or be-
sieged by tough times. We all need help on sunny days and
in sticky times as well. To withhold support, withdraw love,
or remain aloof from persons, particularly when trouble comes,
may be interpreted by them as attack, abandonment, even
alienation. The positive lesson in Christ's analogy is seizing
life's opportunity, responding to the challenge of serviceable
living. To care one must have a gift to give, move into life
with listening love, and confront demonic powers. The call
for help pulls us from carefree pursuits and pushes us to the
edge of crucial needs.

Getting Pushed to the Edge

It is not easy to stir church folk from their daily grind,
heavy preoccupation with work and play, and habitual routine.
Thus, the goal of this chapter is to help each reader develop
a feeling for the human condition.

You may have read the fable of the king who, from his
castle window, observed the people of his kingdom. He became
interested particularly in a cobbler who left his house each
day, walked to his shop, returned home each evening, and
turned out the lights about the same time at night. One day,
as a diversion, the king ordered his royal carpenters to build
a large cage around the perimeter of the cobbler's restricted
routine. Once the cage was completed, the king watched the
cobbler's customary trip from home to shop and back again.
At the end of one year, he requested the cobbler to appear

before him and asked: "How do you like your cage?" to which the cobbler replied, "What cage?"

We might resist this "canary complex" if someone accused us of living in a chrome and velvet cage. One might even prosper in such bondage but, like the serpent feeding on its own tail, eventually the law of diminishing returns wins. Methodist minister William A. Holmes commented on such provincialism: "Surely our salvation must be something more than personal and private, and the authentic life must include the shaping of our existence around the . . . possibilities of our connectedness with other human beings." [1] Provincialism nourishes personal inwardness but fails to reach out beyond one's safe habitat to other persons.

Authentic, timely care must resist not only preoccupation with one's own life but apathy as well. Residents of comfortable suburbs, with fashionable houses and well-manicured lawns, become isolated easily from human needs. What have occupants of golden ghettos in common with tenement dwellers, flophouse people, and old families living in clapboard relics in deteriorated neighborhoods? Theologian Gibson Winter labeled this out-of-sight-out-of-mind condition as "social amnesia," which blinds people to one another's circumstances. [2] What do established executives know of newlyweds, just getting started up the success ladder? What do old couples know of young single adults who group in modest to fashionable apartment complexes? What feelings have blacks for "up and outs" on the city's far north side? What feelings have the new rich for impoverished south-siders? Little, if any. Speeding along city expressways and commuter rails, one is prevented from seeing the garbage-littered lawns, half-nude children, and unpainted shanties of the poor.

A successful businessman had grown sick and tired of the trouble he had experienced with a certain board member. Once he resigned as chief executive officer of the company, he said he could not care for such an enterprise again. "I'm too old and rich to do this all over again," he said. "I'm going

to stay around the lake house and play a little golf and write."
Some people, even at the top, get ground down by life's abra-
siveness and request a long vacation from stress. They may
require considerable help for themselves before moving into
the world again. Provincialism, apathy, and exhaustion take
their toll on potential care-givers.

Life has to push us to the edge of the human condition
to grab our attention, to pull us into the arena of need. One
of the finest ministries I know came about as a result of a
sensitive person's involvement with cancer patients and their
families in the Texas Medical Center. The M. D. Anderson
Hospital and Tumor Research Institute draws patients and
medical staff from across the world. Many patients from out
of the city are referred to some specialist in Houston by family
physicians. They, along with supportive, yet anxious family
members or friends, experience culture shock in a strange city
of nearly three million residents.

A few women in one church were impressed to do something about all the strangers near their gates because they developed a feeling for the condition of cancer victims. Information is provided through religious and social work offices at
M. D. Anderson Hospital that Christian people in Houston
want to help. They are available to assist with housing, transportation, communication, and befriending needs. A telephone
network brings volunteers into touch with special needs and
crisis conditions. The program is several years old and is staffed
seven days a week by volunteers.

An activities center operates each week in that same
church, under the direction of a professionally trained staff.
Programs of education, informal table games, creative arts and
crafts, and recreational activities are offered to members,
friends, and persons needing such resources.

Such ministries permit the church to taste situations and
touch persons outside its Sunday activities. Such caring challenges not simply the relevance of its commitments, but its
very life. It takes church members beyond the boundaries of

present, traditional emphases like Bible study and worship. It moves the congregation beyond the safety of church walls and well-lighted parking areas.

Yet, there are risks to getting involved. When responding to needy persons and circumstances is the basis of churchmanship, some members may feel that traditions are being compromised. When the redemptive word of the gospel stands alongside people in deep need, theological criteria may appear diffused. One must preach more with one's very life blood than with words. To understand and relate deeply to hurting persons necessitates getting near enough to the fire to be burned. Such is the risk of getting pushed to the edge and having to respond.

A Gift to Give

Sensitivity is part of timing in care. Responsiveness is also required if one is to achieve contact with hurting persons and worthy causes. Some people have a problem when religion says, "Forget yourself and live for others," because they are chronically insecure and unfulfilled themselves. This fact lifts up the struggle we all feel between self-centeredness and service, between self-actualization and discipleship. In truth, the right time to care is not only when some need arises but also when one feels dependable and strong enough to offer help.

Swiss psychiatrist Paul Tournier discovered in working with an insecure, unhappy young man that persons must have a *place* before they can leave it and a *gift* before they can give it. He tells of consulting with a patient who came because he could not hold down a job. Although the youth was intelligent and hardworking, he never seemed to fit in with the organization for which he worked. "As a psychiatrist I endeavored to find the root of this problem in his childhood, and I soon discovered that he had suffered . . . from the marital conflict of his parents." [3] His father had been unfaithful to his mother, while she had felt a too-possessive love for her son.

When the couple was divorced, the young man was utterly

confused—full of hatred for his father and distrust of his mother. Instinctively, he started seeking a family or community to take the place of the one he had lost. First he went to the Communists, but in the huge meetings he was always a lone figure.

When he became disillusioned with Communism, he started going about with an existentialist group. He would join them in their close, jam-packed cellars, but no matter how thick the crowd he was still a solitary man. Later, he joined a motorcycle gang that drove around wearing blue jeans, black leather jackets, and crash helmets. Here again he could never feel a part of the group. What emerged, as the young man told his story, was a picture of a person seeking a community, a circle, a substitute family. Yet, because of the wounds which he carried in his spirit, he was unable ever to become authentically incorporated into any group.

"At bottom," the young man reported, "I am always seeking a place." Persons have a great need to have a place, observed Tournier. One must have a place and a people in order to become a person.

The Bible makes much of places—sacred and profane—in the lives of its characters. To Abraham God said: "Go from your country and your kindred and your father's house to the land that I will show you. And I will make of you a great nation, and I will bless you, and make your name great, so that you will be a blessing"(Gen. 12:1–2). Abraham had a place; some people have none. It is to those who have a place that God calls to move on. We need to have a home before we can leave it in a healthy way. To flee home, as did Jacob after obtaining Isaac's blessing in disguise, is to feel oneself a runaway, a traitor, a loner in the earth. We need to receive before we can give. A person cannot offer what he does not possess—including care.

But, one might argue, Jesus had no home. He said, "Foxes have holes, and birds of the air have nests; but the Son of man has nowhere to lay his head" (Luke 9:58). True, his permanent place was not in this world. But the Scriptures teach that Jesus Christ knew who he was, where he was from, and where he was going. He knew "that the Father had given all things into his hands, and that he had come from God and was going to God" (John 13:3). Secure in his identity, vocation, and destiny, our Savior performed his redeeming ministry. This is why he could challenge his disciples to leave their nets and their homes, with the invitation, "Come, follow me!"

The time to care is when one becomes strong enough spiritually to risk being vulnerable to another's wounds. There is a reciprocity between receiving and giving in the divine economy. The twin tasks of gaining selfhood, then surrendering oneself to God appear paradoxical (John 12:25). The Bible calls us to maturity in Christ and commands us at the same time to be like "little children." When one abides in God's grace, he is to abound in generosity (2 Cor. 8:7). One is the input and the other is the output. Receiving and giving are thus inseparable in the Scriptures.

These two movements complete each other and are essential to each other. Discovering one's place and leaving it, *at the divine command,* are not mutually exclusive motions. Sooner or later, we must all leave our places if we are to arrive safely at the one which God has prepared for us. A retiring teacher, for instance, can give the valuable, autographed text editions in his library to selected friends because he cannot keep them forever. Ultimately, all our possessions will be passed along to others. To give one's gifts freely is to choose responsibly the objects of one's concern.

Tournier compared each of God's persons to a trapeze artist. He swings for a while on one trapeze bar and then lets go to catch another. He must have good support from the first bar if he is to have the momentum to gain the second. But finally he must let go if he is ever to reach his goal. The helper's objective is likewise twofold: security for himself, so that he can negotiate the tricky transitions from one trapeze bar to another; and strengthening helpees, so that they can make the leap of faith for themselves.

As one develops a feeling for the human condition and an inner sense of timing, he faces some unique temptations. In each instance they divert the potential care-giver and sidetrack his good intentions.

Temptations that Come a Helper's Way

The incarnational care which I have described thus far implies that love must move into life in order to make a difference. One must offer one's own self—not a set of rules, gimmicks, or a legalistic system—to others as a source of healing. The word *incarnate* is from the Latin *incarnare*—meaning "in flesh"—invested with human nature and form. Incarnate means to embody, personify, realize, actualize as when Jesus Christ became man and other persons "beheld his glory, . . . full of grace and truth" (John 1:14, KJV). When Christ's disciples receive his yoke and "learn from [him]" (Matt. 12:29), they, in turn, embody his saving spirit and redemptive style of love. At least that is the ideal, but numerous temptations stand in the volunteer helper's path.

1. The temptation to run away

People often prefer to leave problems rather than to face and settle them. It is easier to run than to care. I have a psychologist friend who calls this the "approach-avoidance syndrome." One moves toward another individual with real (or feigned) warmth but, when taken up on an offer of closeness, bails out of the relationship. Mobility may become one's preferred life-style in an effort to avoid intimacy.

John Steinbeck, in a unique journey with his dog, Charley, discovered many Americans with an urge "to get away from it all." He reported in *Travels With Charley* that he found a hunger to be on the move in every part of the nation. "People spoke of how they wanted to go someday, to move about, free and unanchored, not toward something, but away from something." [4] Every man, not only Americans, nurtures this dream of leaving the old struggles, hurts, enemies, and frustrations for the challenge of the new. While there is much mobility of the United States population, both into and out of the great cities, we have exhausted the possibility of unlimited space and of unrestricted movement. A person must settle down someday, find his niche, and claim, "This is my place." Hopefully, he will discover life's purpose, something to hope for, work to do, and someone to love.

The German theologian Jürgen Moltmann has commented on the temptation to run away from life's tough decisions and duties. He once observed that the earth has no "new world" for European émigrés. And, in America, moving from one area to another no longer makes any real difference. "The unlimited or infinite lies no longer in space," holds Moltmann, "but in the future, in time. And it is through social transformation that we can now find it." [5] That there is no escape from life will require a radical transformation of our ideals and visions. If people cannot avoid or leave present conditions, there is hope that they can change them. This reality speaks to people professing to care. Rather than avoiding contact by building buffer zones between others and themselves, would-be helpers can construct bridges of relationships in an open future.

2. The temptation to smugness

Jesus warned his disciples against lording their relationship with God over other people. And in the apostle Paul's farewell address to the Ephesian elders, he recalled Jesus' words, "It is more blessed to give than to receive" (Acts 20:35). To be in a position to give to others is fortunate indeed. It is more blessed to possess plenty of money than not enough, health rather than illness, good fortune rather than ill winds. Having to be on the receiving end of financial grants, emotional support, or personal gifts all the time is to feel less fortunate.

America's charity syndrome—Goodwill gifts, Christmas baskets for the poor, and tax write-offs for contributions—encourages a subtle smugness among the givers. It also fosters low self-esteem in receivers who have only gratitude to give in return for material things. Since it is more blessed to give than to receive, the givers are obviously more blessed. This has proved a poor exchange so far as self-image is concerned. Dependent helpees lose face in a transaction in which powerful providers gain self-esteem by their generosity.

The good Samaritan parable is a reminder of potential role reversals. Anyone of us might be the traveler pounced upon by thieves, beaten, and left in a roadside ditch. Someone else might be the helper; we the helpee. We are each subject to disease processes, accidents, social tragedies like divorce, financial reversals, aging, and death.

3. The temptation to simplistic care in a pluralistic society

We were reminded in chapter 1 that care occurs in a world of systems. The church itself is a complex body of interacting believers, in varied denominational structures. No matter how big society is, however, we experience life's crisis points alone. Some individual must care wisely enough to make a difference when deep dilemmas plague life. Where would we be without individuals to visit hospitalized patients, befriend confined prisoners, house the homeless, counsel the confused, encourage the young, comfort the elderly, and bury the dead? Such care is basic; yet, there is more.

To use an analogy from America's past, Where would we be in our attempts to stamp out slavery if only individual efforts had prevailed? How would one worker explain his need for a raise to United States Steel? How would a retiring pilot, without a union, explain his need for benefits to a major airline? The list is endless: women's suffrage, equal employment opportunities, open housing, a minimum wage, fair taxation laws, parity prices in agriculture, competent health care, and so on.

Justice moves through laws and courts to make love's wishes possible. The Lutheran William Hulme wrote that "priestly caring" for personal needs must be accompanied by "prophetic caring" in the social realm.[6] Such an idea is not new since God unites love, power, and justice completely in his own person. We are not to set powerless love against love-less power as polar opposites in human relationships. Such a contrast identifies love with weakness and power with ruthlessness. *Love* is subverted when we think of it only in romantic, sexual, or sentimental terms. *Power* is misunderstood when it is distrusted as universally evil. The late Paul Tillich was nearer the truth by observing that "one is aware of the element of love in structures of power and of the element of power without which love becomes chaotic surrender." [7] Christian *agape*-type love adds something to justice that justice cannot do by itself.

We can see how viewing love and power emotionally, rather than in their basic meanings, distorts communication. Loving enough to act in some sufferer's behalf is basic but not simplistic. To become an advocate for one confined in some prison house of the spirit may require all of the ingenuity, imagination, and intuitive judgment a helper can muster. In truth, our pluralistic culture demands many ways of caring. The bottom line, however, is that we are dependent upon God as the ultimate source of love and power. He is both "loving Father" and "righteous Judge"—the true source of *agape* love and ultimate justice.

4. The temptation to dismiss the high cost of caring

Timely care is most often costly care. Some years ago, a hospitality program for the state's prisoners was arranged in North Carolina. A Baptist couple, responding to their pastor's encouragement, hosted a "model," young male prisoner at worship, for luncheon, and a Sunday afternoon visit. Without cause, the youth shot and killed the man and his wife, was apprehended, and, was indicted later for their murders. The pastor, commenting upon the outrageous crime in their midst, noted that care would continue as long as life lasted. He called the price the couple paid, "The high cost of caring." Such incidents of helpers falling victim to homicidal lust seem endless.

A sixteen-year-old boy who tried to help stop two bicycle thieves, in the Bronx section of New York, was killed by one of the robbers. Police said Henry Schwartz joined in a chase of the thieves after they took an eleven-year-old's bike. The owner of the bike and a twelve-year-old were involved in the pursuit. When Schwartz caught up with the thieves, about two blocks after they abandoned the bicycle because its gears jammed, he told them to wait with him until the other pursuers brought the police. But one of the thieves pulled a switchblade and plunged it into Schwartz's chest. As he fell, struggling, the attacker stabbed him in the back, police reported. Small wonder that heroism comes with a high price tag and that fear for one's own safety holds some would-be helpers back.

To summarize, potential care-givers were invited at the outset of this discussion to develop a feeling for the human condition. Helpers were viewed not as biased, factious answer men, but as persons alert to the questions their imperiled comrades were asking. Timeliness was equated with sensitivity and responsiveness, despite the human tendency to provincialism, apathy, and exhaustion. We noted that one must have a gift to give and a place to move from in order to share human suffering. Finally, we have examined certain temptations that come a helper's way. These may effectively cut off or diminish one's caring capacities and evoke, instead, self-protective maneuvers. Such temptations must be faced in the power of God's Spirit and knowledge of his wise and gracious love (1 Cor. 10:13).

4 The Caring Connection

The church has been pictured thus far as a caring community and laypersons as people who care. We often hear lip service given to the importance of the laity. In truth, the church's real strength lies in its laity—those who belong, attend, pray, give, and back the church with their lives. They are the pastor's force, not merely his field, in ministry. A church's laymen outnumber its ordained clergy. He is one; they are many. While comparatively few laypersons are called to join ranks with the ordained, all ministers have at one time been laypersons. Together, pastor and people form an ideal ministry team.

The average layperson is not always certain what God would have him do. He is not theologically trained; in fact, he may know little about church doctrine and duties. A medical doctor who attended Bible study class every Sunday once said: "You know, most people think that doctors are intelligent. And obviously we do have some intelligence or we couldn't have gotten where we are. But in matters of religion and theology, we stopped growing at the high school level. We just didn't keep up either with the vocabulary or the concepts that would enable us to discuss religious thought with any degree of sophistication."

Pastors, on the other hand, seem to have difficulty understanding the concept of lay ministry. For example, I talked with a staff member of a church who four months earlier had invited me to lead a family life conference for members of that congregation. He and I had planned each learning event—in light of the particular setting, needs and growth di-

46

rections of the church. The conference was aimed at strengthening singles, couples, and family members for life in a tough time.

"The pastor and I have talked," explained the associate six weeks prior to the event. "He says that the church must consider moving to new property soon. It looks like the weekend we had set for the family program is the only time in our schedule when we can feature the relocation issue. Sorry that this conflicts with our conference plans. The pastor will write to you. Meanwhile, be assured that we want you here at the earliest possible date. I'll just keep all the materials you've sent and hope that we can use them later."

Wow! What are the implications of such a cancellation? That structures are more important than persons? That bricks and mortar preclude a focus on family life? How fragile is the present church facility when compared with the fragility of the nuclear family? Since the church has thought about relocating for a long time and has owned new property for three years, why minimize family life in the name of a building campaign? On one particular weekend, the church was going to infuse new life into its volunteers, givers, and workers—not just use them. They were to feel important as single adults, find meaning as teenagers, gain help in relating to spouses, children, and aging parents. All went down the drain for a relocation discussion!

Should families take precedence over facilities in such a case? That depends, but why wait for two or three more years to pass, and a new plant to be constructed, before enriching homelife? It is an old debate: *place* first or *personnel* first—which has priority? Really, human values and housing needs should not be set over against each other. One should not supersede the other; they go hand in hand.

Other churches misunderstand the laity's significance by having a Laymen's Sunday once each year. During the observance, a layperson usually preaches instead of the pastor—often one considering surrender to full-time Christian service. We applaud a midcareer change by a banker, insurance executive, or chemical engineer who decides to "serve Christ" instead of doing secular work. Think of what could be gained by having laypersons, competent in their vocations, to share Jesus Christ at life's interfaces where they are! Why should one feel that he cannot serve Christ in business, medicine, education, or as a homemaker? The apostle Paul taught, "Whether you eat or drink, or whatever you do, do all to the glory of God" (1 Cor. 10:31). And Martin Luther held that all honorable work is acceptable in God's eyes.

Pastoral misperception of laymen searching for new meaning, needing adequate resources for life, and longing to serve God in secular settings is matched by an equally disturbing fact. The church must compete in the marketplace for loyalty and adherence to its doctrines and duties. Many people have been "turned off" by well-meaning, yet unwise, pastors who have attacked them from the pulpit, Sunday by Sunday, rather than undergirded them for life. Others have felt distracted by messages that have little meaning or relevance to the tough, real world where they live and work. Again, church pews are often filled with those who seek comfort and escape from reality. It cannot be assumed that they will respond automatically to invitations, even pleas, to care.

What Churches Can Do

Churches can view caring as a calling for all God's persons for which they must feel gifted (equipped), prepared, and committed. Volunteers who wish to make a caring connection with human needs should be enlisted, trained, and supervised in ministry. Others, equally gifted, will care spontaneously for persons, groups, and structures where there is need. The primary distinction between full- and part-time Christian helpers is not their professional expertise but whether they are paid or volunteer workers.

1. Church people must "hunger and thirst" for right relationships with God and with those to whom they have been sent.

They must want to make a caring connection with people in need. In the preface to his book *Fire and Blackstone,* John Fry of the First Presbyterian Church of Chicago tells of the discoveries he made when he began his ministry in that ghetto section of the city. He walked its streets and alleys, saw the graffiti on the walls, and heard the conversations of gang members on the streets.[1]

He became aware in time that the section of the city in which his church was located had a particular way of looking at life's experiences. The inner city had its own ethos, folkways, language, and values. It had its own areas of concern. If he was to minister there, John Fry had to learn the language and understand the concepts. His responsibility as a preacher was that of interpreter and translator. He did not get the message to be preached from the ghetto, but he did have to find ways to get it into the ghetto.

Perhaps you recall Jesus Christ's eating with some questionable characters. "Some doctors of the law . . . noticed him eating in this bad company, and said to his disciples, 'He eats with tax-gatherers and sinners!' Jesus heard it and said to them, 'It is not the healthy that need a doctor, but the sick; I did not come to invite virtuous people, but sinners' " (Mark 2:16–17).[2] Eventually these close encounters of a caring kind cost Jesus his life. That is why I mentioned the "high cost of caring" in chapter 3. Church people seeking to help others have encountered threats, disappointments, rejection, even fury and bloodshed. Caring at life's interfaces must be done with both eyes open and in a skilled way.

2. The church also functions as an agent of hope in the world.

At a time when many of us teeter close to the brink of despair, the church voices its message of hope and sings hymns of radiant faith. All of this is because of our confidence through Christ's resurrection from the dead (1 Pet. 1:3). Christian hope must be distinguished from shallow optimism or blind faith in some explanation of history that is just not viable. Especially when doctrines are being marketed by religious hucksters, who

sell books and films based on history's perilous end, God's
people must express their confidence in his providential care.
The church's message must be in keeping with reality. We
cannot promise earth's citizens more than life will deliver, but
we can link hands with seekers for a better way. Love can
cut into life and break the bonds of human prisoners. Whatever
the shape of their sin or bondage, ours is a word of good
news about eternal life—here and hereafter.

**3. The church can both test the spirits of those claiming
to be God's spokesmen and wrestle against demonic powers
that enslave life.**

The apostle John taught:"Beloved, do not believe every
spirit, but test the spirits to see whether they are of God; for
many false prophets have gone out into the world" (1 John
4:1). Such an assignment suggests that the care-giver's equipment must be more than skill development. One needs discern-
ment to detect false witnesses, expose them, and see true faith
functioning in life. Second, one should understand signs of
the Holy Spirit's work in salvation, discipline, healing, and
growth. Then, one needs the courage to defy life's demonic
powers through strength in divine grace.

What are some evidences of God's presence in man's pre-
dicament? The Holy Spirit is the creative power of God working
in persons (John 14:26). His touch is immediate. He convicts
of sin and calls persons to right living. God's Spirit overrules
structures that trap persons and shackles that bind them. He
opens up life to Christ and tells us rationally what faith emotionally means. His clash with demonic powers is constant,
while working through God's people "both to will and to do
of his good pleasure" (Phil. 2:13, KJV).

Practicing care puts people in touch with all that is blighted
by evil and suffering. Satan's power exploits life, corrupts motives, destroys relationships, and seeks to usurp God's place.
To be broken, the power of evil must be grasped by a greater
force—the power of God's grace. One certainty, the demonic
was overcome, once for all, in divine redemption. The helper's

job is to make plain what God has done for his creation and to bring release to life's captives.

Courage to break evil's spell and to free anyone trapped in the grip of fate comes from God. He assures us, "You that lodge under the shadow of the Almighty . . . shall find safety beneath his wings" (Ps. 91:1–4, NEB). He alone is with us as we "walk through the valley of the shadow of death." That is why we need fear "no evil" (Ps. 23:4). He is the "God of all comfort, who comforts us in all our affliction, so that we may be able to comfort those who are in any affliction, with the comfort with which we ourselves are comforted by God" (2 Cor. 1:3–4). One has no strength (the biblical word "comfort" means strength) to share until he first receives it from the source of all caring.

4. The church also works on the frontiers of meaning and provides a basis for survival within the social order.

When we pause to think of violated values, lost landmarks, defied laws, and fractured lives in our land, we sense that people must be convinced anew of life's ultimate worthwhileness. People who care hold the secret of life's meaning. Many doubters suspect that the church moves primarily from self-centered motives, that it partakes of modern man's crisis of credibility. People everywhere are searching for some alternative to futility. For religion to become believable God's persons must assert themselves at the frontiers of truth. Since we believe that Christianity is true, we are to practice it (Jas. 2:17). A Christian psychiatrist once spoke of "healing persons in a broken world." That is the caring relevance of the church. We are healers of human brokenness.

Healers of Brokenness

"But how are people hurt around us?" somone asks. "Should we not diagnose ills before treating them?" That is true. The world can crush a man and never know that it has crushed him. Let us think of some ways persons, families, communities, even nations are hurt today.[3]

1. People are hurt by rebellion against God.

There is a radical twist in human nature called sin. This implies that the heart is a rebel, that persons miss the mark of God's purpose, and, worse, that they alienate themselves from him and other people. Sin stains life at every level—personal and social—and separates man from himself, his Maker, and his people. Only divine love has the power to cut into life and to transform it according to God's intended pattern.

2. People are hurt by international conflict and threat of war.

Look around you at news from Third World countries (emerging nations), as well as the superpowers (like Russia, China, and the United States). Military coups may strike suddenly—engineered at times by brilliant, foreign backers. Then a land's history shifts. Spy satellites orbit the earth by day and night, gathering data on military and industrial complexes, and on the location of strategic bases. Dictators ride herd on millions of earth's citizens who have no recourse from their heavy-handed demands. Missionaries serving in foreign lands are often in closer contact with such ruthlessness and bloodshed than are Christians who are safe at home.

3. People are hurt by culture shock—stimuli which threaten our precarious view of reality.

Americans in their forties and fifties have passed into a period of history when they feel almost like strangers within their own land. The good old days are "gone with the wind." Now we face a critical watershed in social history. Liberation movements—among blacks, gays, women, minorities—jeopardize seriously old patterns of relationships. Pornography and permissiveness in sexual mores threaten not merely authority, but survival of institutions like marriage and the family. We have fallen through the cultural curtain of depersonalization into a technocratic society. Demographers tell us how migrations from South to North, from snowbelt to sunbelt, and East to West uproot persons and disrupt relationships.

Still, people need help in coping with social dilemmas, like homosexuality, divorce, and extremism. At a personal level, individuals may have to tune down or turn off some of the stimuli in order to cope. "We must not lose sight of the possibility," notes sociologist Jeffrey K. Hadden, "that man's preoccupation with crisis may paralyze, and otherwise render him incapable of coming to grips with the many problems he faces." [4] On the other hand, faith holds that this sense of urgency may accelerate man's pace toward the fulfillment of his most noble dreams. As a caring community God's people provide practical coping mechanisms—fellowship, acceptance, meaning—for victims of culture shock.

4. Adverse interpersonal relationships in primary groups may do permanent damage to human personality.

A psychiatrist once related the case of a girl born with a caul (fetal membrane) encircling her head. Her superstitious parents believed her to be a witch and reared her as a doomed creature. Her childhood and youth, chained in a tiny, dark room of their apartment, was a living hell on earth. Once discovered by social workers, at about the age of twenty-one, it took years of individual attention and intensive group participation for her to feel like she was a real person.

Someone has said, "For the triumph of evil, it is only necessary for good people to do nothing." Many people respond to depressing circumstances not by despairing, but by doing something to make life better. Christ's example of binding up the brokenhearted and setting free life's captives calls us to minister to deeply troubled people.

5. People are hurt by accidents, diseases, and catastrophes.

Here is a twenty-six-year-old husband and father struck by a fast growing cancer. The doctors perform surgery, cannot remove all of the tumor, yet continue treatments through chemotherapy. We deplore that young man's plight, yet admire his pluck as he holds on to life, prays for remission of the tumor, and seeks strength to work again. To mutiply cases is not necessary; there are millions of such incidents and individuals all about us. Christ's call is to relieve unbearable stress and to share suffering through personal and group mission action.

Churches are obligated to keep the caring vision before people and to challenge Bible study, women's mission groups, and men's groups to become involved in ministry. Task force members are best enlisted one by one and trained for specific missions, rather than invited on a general "everyone come" basis. Volunteer workers must be enlisted, trained, involved, supervised, and affirmed in their helping efforts.

"But the world will not listen to ordinary Christians!" someone protests. To be sure if the world does not listen to the church, often it is because it does not wish to listen to God. Yet, God beckons our belief "Call unto me, and I will answer" (Jer. 33:3, KJV). Blaming the world's indifference on the world is a neat way the church has of justifying itself— of saying, "I'm OK." Likely, it is as much the fault of the church as of the world. Let us confess, the church is not all that she could or should be. Furthermore, we are not free to change without God's convicting and cleansing grace.

If you are one who thinks the church's hands are clean, I would respond that in too many instances the church has no hands. We are care-phobic. Religion is a sweet memory, a happy anticipation, a saintly cult, a stately institution, but not a dynamic community. Anything that happens in the church has to happen locally, though corporate efforts are often needed and worthwhile. A Christian congregation providing acceptance, healing, warm fellowship, and encouragement to face life's overwhelming conditions serves her Lord while helping people (Matt. 25:40).

Converted into the World

There is no way to deal with human suffering without suffering. We read in Hebrews 9:22, "Without the shedding of blood there is no forgiveness of sins." Christ himself is the burden bearer, not we. Yet, as Dietrich Bonhoeffer reminded us, Christians are participants with Christ in his sufferings for the world. Hurting for hurting's sake is not enough. Even "the demons believe—and shudder"(Jas. 2:19). We first are converted (changed) from sin to salvation through faith in God's son. Following growth in discipleship, we need to be converted (channeled) into the world in order for others to believe in Christ and be saved (Matt. 28:19–20).

How can a caring connection be made between a church and objects of need? Where are interfaces for helping our fellowman? The following guide to community ministries was prepared by the Missions Commission of the First Baptist Church, Alexandria, Virginia. Such a guide can help persons and groups with ministry activity plans. It was accompanied by a volunteer enlistment form, with the words: WE NEED YOUR HELP!! at the top. It read:

I am interested in volunteering my services for the following ministries: _____.
Name _____ Age _____
Address _____ Zip _____
Home Phone _____Business Phone _____

Here is the essence of their brochure, entitled "Ministering to the Whole Person," which described community ministries formally supported by First Baptist Church. "Some are thriving, some are struggling, and all offer opportunities for our members personally to extend a Christian hand to people where they are," read the introduction.

WMU—BAPTIST MEN

Woman's Missionary Union and Baptist Men have a responsibility for creating in our church an awareness of the world and its needs. Missions is the curriculum that is studied. Missions is the activity that is carried out. Missions is at the center of their praying and giving.

The age-group organizations were introduced with a number of local mission action activities:

. . . Prisoners are ministered to through the Good News Mission, by grading their Bible correspondence courses, furnishing books for their jail libraries, and assisting in their office work.
. . . Alcoholics and drug abusers are ministered to through the Alcoholism Center, 1401 King Street, Alexandria.
. . . Persons in crisis perhaps are channeled to our church through the Baptist Center.
. . . The sick and the aging are ministered to through nursing homes and hospital visitation and care.
. . . Distributing Bibles, New Testaments, and tracts is a mission project. The WMU and Baptist Men of a church are enthusiastic about involving many people of our church in mission action work. For further information call _____.

Baptist Center

The Baptist Center, at 105 Harvard Street, provides a variety of weekday ministries for residents of the inner city area of Alexandria. The Center sponsors a nursey for preschoolers and clubs for other youth groups, including teenagers. It provides tutoring for younger students and special classes for adults. It helps to meet family emergencies in many ways, including the distribution of food, clothing, and other necessities. The Center's varied programs reach several hundred persons every week. Some of our members find great joy in serving at the Center, but more volunteers are needed. Call _____, Director.

Alive

The heart of ALIVE is a group of Supporting Friends—families who "adopt" a family in trouble and through a continuing effort, on a one-to-one basis, nurture that family to a self-supporting and self-reliant role in the community. The Supporting Friends may call upon other committees in ALIVE, which meet a wide variety of special needs—for housing, furniture, clothing, food, etc. They promote contributions of goods within participating churches and distribute them to the needy.

ALIVE and FISH were started independently of each other by different church laymen in Alexandria, and now they complement each other beautifully—FISH for immediate, temporary help, ALIVE for more sustained or more substantial help. ALIVE'S extensive operations are financed solely by about thirty participating Alexandria churches, including First Baptist. Call the ALIVE office at _____.

Fish

FISH responds to persons who need a friend to help them over a hurdle and don't know where to turn. They call the FISH number _____ at any time. The call is referred to a FISH team captain, who analyzes the situation and arranges for a volunteer team member to perform the needed service. Typical calls are for child care, transportation, shopping or housekeeping for shut-ins, reading to the blind, information and referral services.

First Baptist has good FISH participation with about thirty-five volunteers. A special spirit of fellowship seems to be developing as they share in their interesting and sometimes deeply meaningful experiences. To get more information or volunteer, call the citywide FISH chairman _____.

Fold

FOLD, Inc. is concerned with the care of Alexandria children who are deprived of normal homes because of the death of one or both parents or because their parents are unable or unwilling to provide needed care. The children thus become dependent upon society through no fault of their own. For many children, institutional care is not a good answer. FOLD's mission is to provide what the children need most—a home-type environment. FOLD purchases or leases a house, recruits foster "house parents," and provides material and spiritual support for the new home. Children are assigned by the Alexandria Department of Social Services. First Baptist, along with other churches and foundations, helped to establish FOLD and con-

tinues to support it financially. For more information call
_____.

The Alexandria Community Y

The Alexandria Community Y (not affiliated with YMCA/
YWCA) offers a wide variety of social, educational, cultural,
and recreational programs to the community. Christian volunteers are needed to work in a program for women returning
from mental institutions, jail inmates, crippled and disturbed
children, and alienated teenagers. The Y also needs tutors, driv-
ers, sports coaches, craft and creative sewing teachers, typists,
and musicians. For further information call the Alexandria
Community Y _____.

Good News Mission

Good News Mission is a nondenominational group that
ministers to prisoners and their families. Good News Mission
provides chaplains for jails and prisons; offers a nationwide
Bible correspondence course; distributes literature to prisoners;
operates Opportunity Houses; and provides volunteer opportunities and training with prisoners and their families. For further
information call the Good News Mission at _____.

Family Assistance Room

Under the leadership of _____ the "family assistance
room" has been reorganized and refurbished with new shelves
and facilities for handling clothes. The room will serve as the
center for an increased ministry to the community. You may
bring clothes and toys (in good condition!) and food. These
can best be handled if you will bring them on the first and
third Sundays of each month and leave them in the church
office. The clothing room is now located on the second floor.
Arrangements will be made for distribution to the Baptist Center, ALIVE, or others in special need. For further information
call _____.

Ministry to Internationals

Some Baptist congregations sponsor ministries to internationals jointly with the local Baptist association, state convention, and the Home Mission Board. For example, there are seventy different language groups living in the greater New York City area alone. Some churches select one language group—Spanish, Chinese, Vietnamese, etc.—for a more focused ministry. That is the case with First Baptist Church's Vietnamese Ministry of Northern Virginia, designed to provide witness and ministry to the thousands of Vietnamese living in the area.

Pastor _____, a Vietnamese national, serves as leader of this ministry. Each Sunday from 10:30 A.M. to 12:00 noon, Sunday School groups and morning worship services meet in the pastor's home next door to First Baptist Church. Several other week-day Bible study and prayer groups meet in other areas of Northern Virginia throughout the week. Hundreds of Vietnamese have been touched through programs of pastoral ministry, counseling, Bible study, benevolence, and worship.

Volunteers are needed to assist with the Vietnamese Ministry. Two specific needs that are recurring are prayer for the work and assistance with transportation to and from church on Sunday morning. To volunteer or to get further information on other volunteer needs, please call _____.

Blood Bank Ministry

The First Baptist blood bank plan sponsored by our church provides continuing protection for all of our church families. It provides blood, without cost, to enrolled members and their families. It is not necessary that a family have a qualified donor in order to enroll. Thus, the plan provides blood for those who might not otherwise have this resource. By promoting donorship, First Baptist joins others in a major life-saving program. For further information call the church office _____.

The Deaf Ministry

The deaf ministry of First Baptist Church ministers to the deaf members of our congregation as well as offers services to the large deaf community of this metropolitan area.

An active Sunday School class meets each week and the morning worship services are interpreted for the deaf. There are special events, fellowships, and revivals scheduled throughout the year. Our church provides a Teletype answering service for the deaf. It is operated each morning Monday through Friday from 9:00 A.M. to 12:00 noon by volunteers from First Baptist Church. A Women's Missionary Union circle for our deaf ladies is being formed this year. Deaf ministry is extended through interpreters who assist them in interpreting for counseling, weddings, funerals, medical appointments, and court proceedings, The members of the Deaf Sunday School Class at FBC have taken as a mission project regular ministry to deaf persons in St. Elizabeth's Hospital.

Sign classes are offered periodically for hearing members wishing to learn the sign language for communicating with our deaf friends. For further information call _____.

Special Education

First Baptist Church Special Education Sunday School Department provides Christian education, worship, and fellowship for mentally retarded adults. The program includes Bible study, worship, music, and creative activities. Counseling and consultation is available to parents and family members of the retarded to assist them in living with a mentally retarded child, youth, or adult. _____, a trained and certified teacher, is director. For further information call her at _____.

Mother's Day Out

Mother's Day Out is a child care program for preschoolers that FBC operates. The program, that meets each Tuesday and Thursday, has as its purpose:

. . . To allow mothers of preschoolers "childfree" hours each week for personal activities.
. . . To provide learning opportunities and social experiences for the preschool child in a Christian environment.
. . . To provide an outreach to friends and acquaintances of members of First Baptist Church and to serve the community of which we are a part.

In small groups under professional guidance, preschool boys and girls share experiences of playing, singing, working, and resting in a friendly, cooperative environment. We believe that the love of God must be taught through the everyday experiences of children. For further information call the director _____ or church office _____.

Shared Facilities

The following organizations share FBC buildings and facilities on a regular, on-going basis:
. . . The Mount Vernon Baptist Association _____.
. . . The Pastoral Counseling and Consultation Center of Greater Washington _____.
. . . The School for Contemporary Education _____.

In addition to these a number of community groups include a nursing education group, a childbirth education group, and an ecumenical women's Bible study group.

Whatever the caring connection with varied persons and needs, volunteers must be actively enlisted, prepared, supervised, and affirmed in their service for God. Some directors of the First Baptist Church programs are part-time, paid professionals; most, however, are volunteers. Recruiting workers is a ministry itself—finding healthy, willing persons to fill opportunity slots. Three chief sources of volunteers, noted by professionals in this field, are self recruitment, informal recruitment, and planned recruitment.[5] Each method is a potential source of valuable volunteers.

Workers should bring credentials to caring tasks, like: devoted Christian discipleship; emotional and physical stamina;

love for people; deep faith in God; moral fiber for helping in often trying situations; knowledge of the specific ministry program's purpose, aims, and types of jobs available; enthusiasm about the program; and an ability for dialogue with persons of different backgrounds. Sharing in such programs costs in time, energy, money, and effort—even as Jesus Christ laid down his life for his friends.

Excellent target groups for recruiting volunteers include: WMU organizations, Baptist Men's groups, Baptist Student Unions, Sunday School classes, senior citizen's fellowships, Church Training groups, associational committees, and pastors' conferences. Workers should be truly led by the Holy Spirit and feel called into the caring assignment they accept. In addition, specific caring skills are essential. That is the purpose of chapter 5.

5 Increasing Caring Skills

By now you may be recalling various persons for whom you lacked the courage to care, such as an aged parent who died feeling unloved, a newcomer in your residential area whom you failed to welcome, a business associate who was denied the radiance of your Christian testimony, a child who might have flowered in the warmth of your friendship, or a debtor whom you failed to forgive. The older we grow the more we realize that some goals will never be accomplished. Disappointments and deficiencies are marked, not unfeelingly, into the diaries of our daily lives.

Some failures appear to be final, such as turning from marriage to divorce or from legitimate ambition to delinquent behavior, rebelling against one's own people, violating a cherished value, or abandoning a position for which one has worked all his life. These, at heart, are failures in relationships that cannot be easily explained. Yet failure may not be the end but the beginning of a new phase of development. A psychiatrist encouraged a patient thus, "Your nervous 'breakdown' was actually a 'breakthrough' into new freedom and authentic existence."

Kierkegaard, Danish philosopher of the last century, once observed about Christians, "In his failure the believer finds his triumph." This was true of the apostle Paul who, though persecuted, confessed, "I want you to know, brethren, that what has happened to me has really served to advance the gospel" (Phil.1:12). So often we learn best not by winning but by losing. Thus God can carve out a new channel in which one's life may flow toward the immortal sea of his divine purpose. One who has been comforted by God's Spirit can never doubt the grace that claims him, though his life is spent in greater mystery.

You recall the qualities of caring persons mentioned thus far: (1) *agape* love, (2) sensitivity to human needs, (3) a gift to give, (4) faith and fiber as tokens of spiritual toughness and strength, and (5) the peace of God by which we have been comforted in our own failures and grief experiences. These marks of maturity are relative achievements in Christian experience—goals toward which we strive. Browning was right, "A man's reach must exceed his grasp." Attention moves now to enhancing caring skills in order to prevent other opportunities from slipping through our fingers.

Are You Available?

One pastor I know spends about twenty-five hours each week in diligent sermon preparation. He preaches well-polished messages, containing numerous quotations and apt illustrations. But he visits rarely with people inside of or outside of the church. In fact, he is contacted only in emergencies which staff members cannot handle.

Is there anything wrong with having a little privacy, whether at work or at home? Definitely not. You must have some time alone for personal grooming, spiritual growth, private conversations, needed rest, and creative labor.

I am speaking here, however, of the skill of accessibility— making oneself available to family members, fellow workers, students, clients, colleagues, patients, or church members. While there is room for all kinds of persons in the ministry, including the scholarly recluse, there is also a *need for a presence*— a pastor who cares for people—in our churches.

Protestant pastors often feel caught in a professional trap. There are sermons to prepare, sick folk to visit, prospective members to enlist, civic affairs to support, bulletins to compose, reports to submit, committees to attend, plus anxiety over inadequacy, guilt over failure, hostility toward criticism, and never enough time. The wife of a downtown minister said during a Wednesday night dinner at church, "My husband and I have had dinner together alone only one time this entire month." Psychiatrist Louis McBurney is right. *Every pastor needs a pastor* in order to find freedom and fulfillment in ministry.

Pastors and people can be too busy at church to deal with vital issues. God does not require our busyness, only our faithfulness in living the gospel wherever we are. We must continually break out of institutional modes of thinking into personal and small group relationships.

Finding more time to be available to persons in need is a problem for laymen, not just ministers. For example, a patient in psychotherapy, paying fifty dollars a visit, became discouraged when her psychiatrist kept falling asleep during counseling sessions. Thinking that he was tired at 4:00 P.M. each Thursday—her hour—she rescheduled appointments at 10:00 A.M., earlier in the week. But, to her dismay, the therapist still napped while she poured out disappointments, snags, and failures in her life story.

Was she a bore? or was the doctor a tired old man? Whatever the answer, that professional care-giver in accepting a client entered a covenant of faithfulness with her to strengthen insight and responsibility. She felt rejected, and rightly so, because the door of his attention (not his office) appeared closed.

To open oneself *in Christ's spirit* to a neighbor's spiritual lostness, moral confusion, shattering crisis, or social need can be a costly action. Such accessibility may be spontaneous or intentional, yet generosity cannot be programmed. When I need privacy, a time clearly apart from the demands of people who call or come into my office, it must be arranged. I have discovered that any hour my office is open, hurting people are standing at the door, waiting to visit.

How can others know that you are there and that you care—in family relationships, for example?

Parents can increase their accessibility to their own children by spending some time during the week (daily if possible) with each of them. Many young parents want to get away from their children and let the baby-sitter take over. God gave children two parents for a purpose. They need a father—a masculine person with whom to identify—as well as a mother. A growing child looks upon adults as all-powerful, mysteriously wise, and financially stable. Of course, they shed such illusions in adolescence and see the inconsistencies and human flaws of both parents. Still, boys and girls like to talk with grown-ups about many things: God, the world, animals, their brothers or sisters, school, sex, suffering, even the characters in their favorite bedtime stories.

Care Requires Involvement

Already, you see that accessibility is more a matter of spirit, a helpful disposition, than of sitting in an office waiting for a knock on the door. Care takes the initiative, makes a call, sees a need, acts on a generous impulse to help. Consider the following example.

An elementary school teacher, who worked with socially deprived children, was riding home from work one afternoon with her husband. "Charles," she said, "I want to run by Rich's and buy little Sherry some casual shoes."

"Sherry who?" he replied.

"You know! She's one of the youngsters from the Hope Children's Home who was transferred to my room in January."

"Those kids are always needing something," Charles answered disgustedly. "They're either sick or in some kind of trouble. I wish you wouldn't get involved with them!"

Do Christians have a right to avoid getting involved with people in trouble? Christ was always "taking a towel and girding himself" in order to minister to others and to set an example for believers. Just as he preached "deliverance to the captives" in the days of his flesh, he works through Christians in order to bring hope to men today. That elementary teacher knew the plight of a child who needed shoes like the others in her classroom wore. So she purchased them and presented them in a moment of privacy to a youngster trapped by the divorce of parents, neither of whom wanted her.

How different such a generous disposition is from that of laymen who constantly expect favors from friends or ministers who know someone who can "get it for them wholesale."

Along with incidental, casual, and spontaneous opportunities for service, churches will plan specific ways to meet varied needs. Planned activities may touch lives of outsiders: singles (including formerly married persons), internationals residing in America, patients in hospitals, residents of convalescent centers, or physically handicapped citizens like the deaf. On mission fields classes are offered in culinary arts, home nursing, child care, sanitation, literacy, and varied crafts, as well as Bible study. Special programs, with pastoral intent, may be conducted with persons or groups in the church.

One church planned a "cues for college" day with all graduating high school seniors. It was a guidance program of orientation in a recreation center which afforded decorative surroundings, a delicious luncheon, and swimming privileges, in addition to four dialogue sessions. The basic purpose of the effort was to expose students planning to attend college to the academic, social, and religious atmosphere of the modern campus, under the direction of capable Christian educators. Imagine the sense of significance that those young people experienced as they talked with top personnel about varied areas of college life. Fears and frustrations came out in the small groups. Information displaced illusions. The promise of monthly mailings of a Christian student publication and pledges of friendship from adults in the educational power structure encouraged all of the participants.

It will take several years to evaluate the effectiveness of such efforts, but the initial response of students and staff was excellent.

Communicating Concern

Assuming your willingness to risk encounters with alien persons—to be accessible—how can a layman build bridges between the church and the world? Personal piety is honorable, but merely being a proper Christian is inadequate when one sees his neighbors fighting for survival, victimized by suffering or injured by cruel social forces. Neither can we be indifferent when crises like illness or death come. People are weak and need God's help. The best way to learn what their real needs are is by listening and responding to the facts and feelings that they express.

For example, Howard West, a barber shop owner, once shared a family grief experience with Bud, one of his employees. Howard's son, Max, and daughter-in-law, Doris, had a baby son born with a congenital heart defect. This was the Wests' first grandchild, born with only half a heart. Kirk died within six weeks after birth, and the Wests were plunged into grief for themselves and their son.

About a month after the infant grandson's death, the Wests entertained Bud. His wife was visiting her family out of state. According to Bud, the following is a partial account of their conversation after the evening meal. Bud inquired about Max and Doris. Mrs. West brought in some pictures of little Kirk then returned to the dishes in the kitchen.

HOWARD: Doesn't he look good? You would never guess that he had a sick day in his life. *(Note his grandfatherly pride.)*

BUD: He really does look healthy. *(Shortly, Mrs. West returned to talk with them.)*

MRS. WEST: Doesn't the baby look so sweet?

BUD: Yes, he does. He looks like a normal healthy baby, as I just told Howard.

MRS. WEST: Well, he acted healthy too. He would kick and move about in the incubator. He was really active to be so sick. It was nice of you men at the shop to send flowers to the service. Here are some of the beautiful flowers that people sent. Aren't they pretty? *(The room was crowded with potted plants.)*

BUD: Yes, they are. *(Mrs. West spoke of Doris and of people's kindnesses.)*

BUD: I suppose Max and Doris are about settled down from this experience.

MRS. WEST: Well, of course, Max is right back in the groove of school, and I suppose Doris has become adjusted to it also. Really, we are all just now getting out from under the pressure of it. It was so very hard for awhile. Howard and I would talk about little Kirk every day, wouldn't we, Howard?

HOWARD: Yes, we would. But we decided that we would have to stop living in the past. I guess you call it that, don't you? It doesn't bother us to talk about it now. It was just one of those things you would like to forget. At least, we don't think about it all of the time.

BUD: Do you think that there was purpose in it all? What I mean is, do you think that it happened for any particular reason?

MRS. WEST: Well, my minister said there was a reason.

HOWARD: Of course, we can't see why or the reason now. Maybe later we will. We first thought that perhaps it was because Max was still in school and a child would just have been another burden on them. But we felt also that the loss of a child would be a heavier burden, so that idea didn't make any sense to us. We now feel like this is all God wanted and that it is all for the best.

MRS. WEST: What's the Scripture in Romans that Brother Polk our minister read to us?

HOWARD: I don't remember. It's something about everything is for the best to the children of God. Do you know what verse it might be, Bud?

BUD: Yes, I know that Scripture. "All things work together for good to them that love God" (Rom. 8:28, KJV).

HOWARD: Yes, that's it. That's all we can say now.

MRS. WEST: Isn't it wonderful how one verse like that can set your mind at ease?

BUD: Yes, it is wonderful. That's the power of God's Word. It is always sufficient for our every need.

HOWARD: Well, I know one thing. This experience has taught me how weak we are and how much we need other people. You really discover who your friends are when something like this happens.

MRS. WEST: You sure do. And another thing, Max and Doris have been to church together every Sunday since the funeral. He used to not go because he needed to study. At least they go to the morning services now.

BUD: You are seeing some purpose in it already.

HOWARD: You just never know, do you? I mean, this thing is so rare. The doctor said that only one out of every ten or twenty thousand births occur with this type of heart defect. There must be a real good reason for those odds to fall on us. You just never know.

MRS. WEST: But we do know that God loves his children. He knew it would be better to take little Kirk home than to let him suffer so much here on earth.

BUD: Yes, that's right. God doesn't like to see any of us suffer. *(Thereafter, the conversation drifted off to other areas, news affairs, and so on.)*

Later, in reflecting upon the conversation, Bud noted his anxiety about using religious language with the Wests. He was afraid to "talk spiritual," as he put it. Yet, God's Spirit was evident during their visit. Howard and his wife spoke freely of their grief and disappointment precisely because their guest was a good listener. This family was independent and resourceful. Yet they discovered that, upon occasion, people need other people and God desperately. When the matter of *purpose* was mentioned, the Wests clarified what their gains— human and divine—from the experience had been. True, Bud did not say much but what he said supported the Wests' disrupted value system and permitted them to verbalize God's revelation through the death experience.

Can you improve your capacity as an understanding Christian communicator? What can be learned from clinical evidence in the above visit?

1. You may have little control over an interview, for you talk with numerous people every day. As in Bud's case, you can counsel persons with whom you have a relationship of mutual trust and confidence. Some people find it easier to talk with a stranger than with a close friend. You may have an opportunity to be that stranger.

2. Therapeutic (healing) conversations cannot be forced upon a "prospect." You can take the initiative by making yourself available to another person, but he must desire to share himself with you in the presence of God.

3. The time and place of your conversation should afford discreet privacy, emotional freedom, and unhurried affection for the person or family. A physician, for example, who is related formally to his patients will talk with them in an office setting. Whereas, you, as a friend making an informal visit, will talk with persons at home, on an airplane, or in a wayside place like a store.

4. You may not have all the answers. Bud's role was that of a Christian friend and employee. He did not play God by

aggressively controlling the conversation, voicing judgment upon Max and Doris for poor church attendance, or explaining why Kirk died. He disavowed the role of a judge or a minister in favor of the role of friend.

5. The helper did not try to carry the West's burdens for them. In the spirit of Galatians 6:1–5, Bud shared their burdens and transferred their dependency needs onto God "from whence cometh our help" (see Ps. 121:1–4, KJV). This is true pastoral care in that the individual or family is permitted to grow through suffering in the power of God's Spirit.

6. Through laypersons, God places a "priest at every elbow." The late Baptist theologian Carlyle Marney quoted Martin Luther thus, "Every baptized Christian is . . . a priest." [1] The pastorhood of the laity, through which men are truly neighbors to one another, is not an antipreacher movement. Rather, it is a realization of how Christ's body—the church—functions at many levels of human interconnectedness.

Along with these lessons about communicating concern, here are some guidelines for laymen to follow in counseling experiences.[2] They are listed without comment because their meaning is clear.

1. Prepare your heart daily through prayer in order to present God to any individual or family in need.

2. Respect the helpee. Be interested in him as a person, not just curious about his problem.

3. Consider the problem as important. Don't belittle or mock an individual regardless of the problem's nature.

4. Remember that suffering people are sensitive, often hostile, so be patient no matter how superficial, halting, or shocking the story.

5. Resist the temptation to pry into unrevealed secrets.

6. Let the counselee use his own words, assume responsibility for his own actions, and make his own decisions.

7. Be willing to admit that you do not have or need to have all of the answers.

8. Explore acceptable alternatives without attempting to convert a person to your point of view. Of course, in evangelistic visitation, you will keep the conversation Christ-centered using appropriate Scripture passages.

9. Watch your spirit. Try not to be defensive or argumentative in response to the person's words or basic attitudes. It is easy to become impatient or abrupt.

10. Share with the person until a course of action is settled upon, or make additional time for another interview if that seems necessary.

Listening and responding to facts and feelings of other people is not an inherited quality. Sharing another's plight and pilgrimage is a learned experience. Some people need a course in remedial listening. Others should practice keeping confidences. Do not expect someone to bare his soul, share secret sins or hurts, unless you intend to share something of yourself. *Your interest and comradely care will prove more effective than giving advice or rejecting a worrier.*

Visiting Is Witnessing Too

Some people spend their lives preparing to live, intending to serve God and mankind. They never plunge into the adventure. Like the character in Russell H. Conwell's famous story *Acres of Diamonds,* some persons think that if they were living in some other place or had entered another vocation, they would have more success. You may recall that the man sold his farm and sought his fortune out in the world. In time, the farm's new owner discovered tiny stones shimmering in the sun—stones that later proved to be diamonds. Had the original owner looked carefully at his opportunity he would have possessed a fortune in gems.

Visiting is like that. The layman who waits for "one shining moment in history" to testify of his faith in God will likely never visit in the church's behalf. There is much to be said for a social call which is simply a friendly visit with a neighbor or newly arrived family in your city. Not every visit will be devoted to discussing theology, the church, or personal problems. You don't have to look for trouble when calling in Christ's name. It will show up soon enough.

Take the case of a lady who began visiting women in the local jail, then started a Bible class for inmates.

"Reading my Bible sent me scurrying to jail!" confessed Mrs. Debbie Royal. "The words I read were the words of Jesus, 'I was sick and you visited me, I was in prison and you came to me'" (Matt. 25:36). She took Christ seriously.

Recalling her early impressions of the county jail, Mrs. Royal described the bare floors, barred windows, bleak walls, and the unsavory looking characters in the jail. She was more shocked, however, with female prisoners who spent wearisome days on their bunks. Only a spoon was permitted for eating. No furniture was permitted except the iron bunks. The prisoner's faces bore horrible signs of bitterness and sin. One woman, about forty, had a scar on her forehead and tattoos on each arm. There were drug addicts, alcoholics, prostitutes, and first offenders, including one girl who was pregnant out of wedlock.

The Christian visitor taught them Bible lessons each Monday, carried them literature, food, her love, and her Savior. She was attracted to the unwed, expectant mother who said that she wanted to keep her baby. "I want one thing that is really mine to love. My father ruined me because of drink. My mother would not believe me. After that I never cared what happened." Later, she admitted that adoption was best but asked that the infant be placed with a nondrinking couple.

Mrs. Royal confessed that she had never had any training or experience to prepare her for work in a jail. "I do not like, humanly speaking, to visit the jail. But I love the Savior. I want to follow his footsteps wherever they may lead me. I have found that people in jail are just people too. They are people who need to know the Savior."

We may conclude that loving interest in and concern for people is the basic purpose for church visitation. There may or may not be a major crisis. Yet, even in social calls, one

should have a reason for calling and trust God's Spirit to prepare the way for a redemptive relationship.

Experienced visitors can help the beginner to avoid superficial contacts and wasted trips. Specific guidance for hospital
calling will be provided in a later chapter. Here are some guidelines for visiting persons with pastoral intent.

1. By carrying the church to people you are free to meet
on their own ground, see them in the context of daily experience, and to understand their outlook upon life.

2. Prepare for calling by checking areas of the city in which
you accepted an address or assignment. Apartment addresses
can be especially confusing when several buildings that look
alike are clustered together.

3. A time for visiting will be determined by your own
schedule and that of the person with whom you shall get acquainted. Some visitors telephone in advance, not just to make
an appointment, but to make certain the family or party will
be at home.

4. While company in calling—like your wife, a friend,
deacon, or staff member—is not essential, it is often helpful.
Two separate pictures of a situation are obtained. One caller
offsets errors in judgment or false impressions of another visitor. Some potential church members will admit a couple into
a house or apartment but would refuse admittance to a single
man.

5. Begin graciously with the person for his own sake. Say
a positive word about the family, the house, or its furnishings.
Get to know the person by listening to his religious background, family interests, work concerns, hobbies, and so on.
Circumstances will dictate whether you should use the Bible
and prayer. Stay long enough to accomplish your purpose but
do not prolong the discussion. If records are desired by your
church office, these should be provided for the sake of other
visitors that follow you.

Someone may reason that visitation is the pastor's job.
You may hear a fellow church member say "That's what we're

paying Harry to do." It is likely that the total task of pastoral care of all the church's members and prospective members will exceed the capacities of both pastor and staff. You may share the age-old task of calling upon newcomers, the sick, aged, shut-ins, nonmembers, and bereaved persons for the glory of God.

Praying for Others

Many church members feel so helpless when news comes of persons or groups needing help. They obtain information but fail to act. This feeling about one's involvement in crucial situations has already led us to a consideration of what one person like yourself can do: make yourself available, understand through conversations, and dare to witness through visitation. Logically, we come now to consider how prayer can help others.

The New Tetament makes much of the practice of prayer in behalf of persons in need. Portions of our Lord's prayers are threaded into the Gospels (Matt. 6:9–13; John 17). He instructed his disciples to pray privately, not publicly as did the hypocritical Jews (Matt. 6:6). Jesus spent long hours in communion with his heavenly Father (Mark 1:35; 6:46; Luke 5:15; 6:12). In the garden of Gethsemane, Christ implored that if it were his Father's will, the cup of suffering might be withdrawn (Luke 22:42).

Some moderns think that prayer—vital communion with God who has spoken to us in printed and living Word—is a waste of time. They conclude that God has predestined all things to happen, so why pray? From man's side, prayer appears to be his effort to release resources in his behalf which are beyond his control. Yet, from God's side, prayer is a grace gift—his promise to listen, to understand, and to act in behalf of any true believer. This is why he commanded prayer for and by the saints (1 Chron. 16:11; Hos. 14:2; Matt. 7:7; Luke 18:1; John 16:24; Eph. 6:18).

Christians have this certainty: God does answer prayer.

Numerous promises of answers to prayers are found in the Scriptures. The disciples were instructed to pray in "Jesus' name"—meaning that they were to live, not merely speak, in obedience to him (Luke 11:9; John 15:7). Through obedience members of the early church were blessed by God's Spirit, and many persons were saved and healed (Acts 1:14; 4:24; Jas. 5:15–16). Prayer exerts an influence upon God's action, even upon his existence. This is what the word *answer* means.

How does God answer us? The foundation of our prayers centers in Jesus Christ. If his words truly "abide in" us, he shall intercede continually as our high priest (Heb. 10:19–21), and we may expect God's response (1 John 3:22). This assurance increases our faith and steadies our hands for tasks that we can do. Admittedly, there is much mystery in prayer, for God remains free to act as he wills. Yet, he listens to us. John the apostle envisioned angels mingling incense with prayers "and the smoke of the incense rose with the prayers of the saints from the hand of the angel before God" (Rev. 8:4). This is the ground of Christian assurance.

In Christ, God taught us how to pray, and through his Spirit he participates in the anxious longing and joyous thanksgiving of his children. The Holy Spirit intercedes with God himself when overwhelmed Christians do not know how to pray or what to say (Rom. 8:26).

How shall we pray? Posture in prayer makes little difference; it is the believer's attitude that counts. He must humble himself before God. We do not have to shout or use holy words. What matters is that God listens, not that our words are forceful. We must think of *him,* not preach to auditors who may overhear our words. Effective prayer is appropriate to the occasion, whether carefully planned or spontaneous, natural in tone, and offered in a spirit of reverence. Some persons prefer to write out their prayers with carefully chosen phrases, as did David, the psalmist, long ago.

There are prayers for special occasions, like the dedication of a new worship center, and as part of public worship. Here, for example, is a prayer I offered in the chapel of Southwestern Baptist Theological Seminary one spring morning.

Our dear Father, we turn to you out of the sheer need to pray—for ourselves and all of the others: *newborns,* the freshest gifts from your hands that we know; *friends, spouses,* and *intimates,* who share life's passages and make tolerable its turning points and tough times; *parents* back home, who have believed in us when we could not even believe in ourselves; *teachers,* who prepare faithfully for close encounters of the classroom kind; and *students,* who have grown weary in well doing.

Thank you, God, for nature's nursery season when all the world is young again; for a hundred tints of green, yellow, white, pink, lavender; and for the promise of new life.

Thank you, God, for calling us to witness and work in ten thousand vineyards across the world:

. . . in day care centers, with little children;

. . . in youth ministries, where the young search for identity;

. . . in churches, Bible studies, recreation, and the arts;

. . . and here, at Southwestern Seminary, where the day's duties require faith and fiber.

Now, amid sounds of the sanctuary, songs of praise, and a message from your eternal Word, *save us* from fear and insecurity as old structures lose their power; *spare us* from persons who absolutize their views, feelings, and experiences and project them as 'gospel' across our nation; *forgive us* our sins of sanctimoniousness, deceitful devotion, and pious idolatry; and *free us* from the peril of cuteness with holy things and curtness with your people.

Speak your message to this assembly and send us forth to live courageously in a violent land. We pray through Christ our Lord. Amen.

How does prayer help? In John Baillie's words, prayer helps us to "sense the presence of God." We are to place our trust in God, not in our words. A woman once said to evangelist C. E. Autrey, "I've lost my faith in prayer." She explained her doubts and said that her words were not getting out of the room. "The problem," he responded, "is that you are not truly trusting God." Prayer reminds us of things we have forgotten and causes us to relax our desires into greater plans than our own. Prayer helps us to gain perspective. It enlarges our vision and expands our concern. Prayer sensitizes us to the needs of others, as well as ourselves. We are strengthened by the fellowship of other trusting people who pray, as well as by the witness of the saints in the Bible.

You may be thinking about those dark times in your life when God heard your requests for health or success or family unity—yet said no. Nothing disappoints us more than feelings of optimism or complacency when conditions do not warrant it. With God "all things are possible." Yet, from the human point of view some things are impossible. God, however, answers his children in one of two ways. He answers our *request* and grants the petition; or he answers the *believer* while refusing his request. In either instance, God's true child is reinforced for life. He can say, "In his will is my peace."

There are varied ways through which the church's fellowship may be extended to persons facing life's hazards, decisions, and responsibilities that we shall not discuss.

Two matters merit brief mention here, however. The first concerns your keeping in touch through correspondence or telephone calls with persons who mean much to you or who rely upon your friendship. Time and distance separate persons and families today. Yet occasions like birthdays, anniversaries, weddings, and commencements offer opportunities to express interest in friends of all ages. I know one lady who composes poetry with a specific person or occasion in mind then sends a copy to the honoree. Personal notes may be written in your own hand thanking friends or relatives for gifts or a visit, expressing appreciation to some civic leader or teacher, or assuring a sick friend of your concern. Where personal visits or telephone calls are impossible, with foreign missionaries for example, a message can be mailed inexpensively. A letter represents focused spirit and can strengthen emotional bonds between other persons and counselees.

The complexity of human needs today requires consideration of a final matter—referring persons in special situations to specialists who have the education or organized resources commensurate with the problems involved. Social, medical, legal, and public welfare resources are made available to all citizens regardless of race or religious affiliation. There are persons—like delinquents, sex deviates, criminals, the severely retarded, and mentally ill—whose limitless needs can quickly overtax the resources of one person, family, or congregation.

Such situations call for a nonroutine approach, for professional experience in coping with persons in such circumstances, and for organized resources that guarantee continual, even long-term, assistance if it is required. Do not count it a personal failure when some person's or group's need lies beyond you. Be wise enough to consult ministers, physicians, legal aid officials, educators, and social workers who are trained to cope with desperate situations.

6 The Ministry of Friendship

Ours is the age of plastics—of fragile substitutes for materials like steel, wood, and precious stones. We have accustomed ourselves to printed circuits rather than copper wire, to disposable tissues rather than linen handkerchiefs, and to television images rather than live personalities. This is the era of plug-in/plug-out people—where one junior executive is as good as another, grocery clerks are unknown computer operators at a checkout stand, and uniformed servicemen repair household gadgets for a fee of one dollar a minute. All ties appear tenuous. Social occasions are gauged by their conviviality and deafening conversation level rather than by standards of true relationships. We lament that friendship, one of humanity's greatest blessings, is sadly out of fashion.

Suddenly, a new executive comes on the scene, transferrred from an office a thousand miles away. We hear that his administrative assistant will soon be following him, after he sells his house and sets things in order. While some business leaders run through two or three assistants each year, we learn that this man and his colleague have worked together for almost a decade. They have discovered a depth of meaning in working side by side and a degree of mutual care and support that frees them through togetherness. Such exceptions to the general practice of treating employees like disposable products reminds us that life without true friends is hardly life at all.

This is a book about care, about *agape* love in action. Ironically, it seems easier to care about citizens in a foreign land than about one's roommate or fellow students or boss. There is little use in training ourselves to care for the others (out

81

there) unless we are willing to befriend those family members, work associates, and neighbors near at hand.

The ancients viewed friendship as the happiest and most fully human of all ties—the zenith of life and a school for character. The modern world, in comparison, ignores it. We admit that, besides a spouse and children, a person needs a few friends. But the term itself implies casual associates, like a barber or beautician, and social acquaintances rather than abiding friends. Someone said: "I can count my true friends on the fingers of one hand. I have numerous acquaintances with whom I feel congenial, but that's a different feeling from friendship." A real friend—like a pearl of great price—is rare. Why is this so? Perhaps few persons value friendship because few experience it.

I know numerous individuals in church life, some in executive positions, who are gifted at using people. They have asked favors, borrowed ideas, called for help, requested extra effort, and scrambled over the shoulders of countless associates on the way to the top of the ecclesiastical status heap. We are well acquainted with folks whose need-love outruns their gift-love by many miles. They are long on expectations, on taking, but short on generosity, on giving in return.

Friendly people are everywhere today—easy at introducing themselves, giving you the dubious gift of their first names within minutes. For example, I sat down by a stranger on a DC-9 jet, and momentarily the flight attendant was by taking orders. "Let me buy you a drink," offered the stranger. I declined but introduced myself to a labor union official from Miami, Florida. Such individuals never really invite you in behind their wandering eyes and half-smiles where the real person lives. Friendship is not, for them, a relationship of great value but a useful commodity to be shopped for like toothpaste or deodorant.

Such glibness is a far cry from friendship as William Penn saw it—"a union of spirits," a "marriage of hearts"; or as the philosopher Montaigne envisioned it—"one soul in two bodies." How far does friendship go on a scale from I-barely-know-you to companionship to marriage mates? And what of God's friendship with man and our God-consciousness in an age of uncertainty? Some persons may need a little encouragement or guidance in the skill of friendship formation. Others may need assistance in getting out of a sticky, even unhealthy, relationship. All of us need help in managing occasional feelings of loneliness.

The Shape of Loneliness

Here, I am distinguishing *solitude,* life's self-chosen times of aloneness, from *loneliness*—feeling cut off from the human community. We each need a private sanctuary of the spirit into which God alone is invited. The art of detachment, of quietness, of prayer can be cultivated whatever the living conditions or circumstances about us. Aloneness is something we need to accept and enjoy. One who is at ease with himself will feel more at ease with others. Togetherness with God can strengthen one's capacity for all other relationships.

Loneliness, on the other hand, is the emotional opposite of shared life together. It implies noncommunication, shutupness, solitariness, isolation, deprivation—where people and experiences of great value are missing. Think for a moment about the burden of loneliness which many persons feel: the very rich and the very poor, powerful and powerless individuals, high achievers and sorry failures, adolescents and their middle-aged parents, homebound persons, victims of deafness and blindness, single and divorced persons (and the children of divorced parents), those at the top who must produce to survive, and those at the bottom who must depend upon their productive fellow citizens. The list seems endless, and the burden is great.

Loneliness may accompany narrow scrapes and feelings of grave crisis. I recall the experience of some families who had chosen to travel together during a summer vacation. On an outing near Chattanooga, Tennessee, several of their children wandered into an unexplored cave without adult supervision. The grown-ups cleaned up after their picnic, enjoyed hiking and conversation, then discovered that some of their children were lost. The fact that they had not come back out of the dark cave—laughing, with flashlights beaming—chilled their parents' spirits. Calling their names at the cave's entrance brought no response. Mothers panicked, fearing the worst (like a son falling into a bottomless pit or a daughter drowning in an underground stream).

The parents, aunts, and uncles were all there but without their children they felt alone. All that they had sacrificed for their offspring through all the years flashed suddenly through their minds.

Appalled by the approaching night, their circumstances seemed unreal. Help was called—an old timer from the area who knew the cave—and a search was begun. In time, just as the children had wandered excitedly away from their parents to explore the caverns, they reappeared. All were safe. A sense of separation, which had held their parents in the grip of fear all afternoon, was overcome in joyous reunion. An accidental separation increased each parent's and child's appreciation of the worth of companionship. Their emotional bonds were strengthened precisely because they had experienced the shadow side of solitude.

One of the beautiful things about parenting children is the discoveries which love makes along the way. We have no clan or tribal loyalties, no fixed community life, to tie us together in Western society. Ideally, the emotional bond between parents and children deepens into friendship with the passing of time. A man described a conversation he had overheard between a mother, in her thirties, and her sixteen-year-old daughter, "They sounded more like sisters talking than a mother and child." Friendship like that may seem more precious by its absence than by its presence in many families.

"A friend in need is a friend indeed," goes an old adage. That is more true today than ever before; we all need help along the way. For example, during a drive to a neighboring city one winter evening, a friend blew out an automobile tire. He was alone. No flashlight was in the car. It was after dark and cold. No one was sensitive enough to stop and aid him while he changed tires in the darkness. He discovered the absence of relationships—what traveling alone and having difficulty could mean—rather than the richness of association through that experience.

You may have known of people in similar circumstances being attacked, not helped, by a passerby; or of a woman being raped, not befriended, by some malicious maniac. Such malevolence reveals the sterility of relationships, selfishness of social misfits, and sin of brutal lust in modern life.

How different the experience of a woman who had a flat automobile tire one rainy afternoon. She was returning home after visiting her aged mother in the country. "Two different men, driving in the opposite direction from my car, stopped, turned their cars around, and came and helped me," she told her son. Such care may have been motivated from mere chivalry or good neighborliness rather than charity. Still, compassion is alive in the earth, and people do befriend strangers with no thought of credit, praise, or reward.

The burden of loneliness can become too great for some young people to bear. Adolescence is a tumultuous time, marked by physiological changes, psychic turbulence, and social upheaval.[1] A girl on the way to womanhood needs befriending by competent parents and caring peers. A son needs the security of a true father's love as the sparks of independence fly between them. He also needs special friends to help him negotiate life's tricky passages into adulthood.

I recall the experience of a seventeen-year-old youth's suicide, by hanging, one Saturday afternoon. The son of a successful automobile dealer, his family had everything (except the main thing). The father was a heavy drinker, an indecisive man, who leaned on his wife for emotional strength and economic support.

No note was left by the boy. Neighbors suspected foul play at first or drug abuse. Neither cause was established. What does one say to parents whose only son has said no to life and chosen a separate path? Shallow explanations for suicide will not do. The time for companionship is before trouble comes, not after the fact, hopefully preventing such a sad escape from life's risks and responsibilities. Once a child has died by his own hand, parents spend the rest of their lives in greater misery.

The bonds of loneliness may be broken by friendship. Who could be more isolated than a homebound, eighty-nine-year-old woman, severely deaf, partially blind, with no driver's license? Totally dependent upon others to take her shopping, to church, and to her doctor, that woman understood loneliness. Mrs. McLain referrred to the lady who came by each week and took her shopping."She's a good friend of mine," she explained. "I don't know what I would do without her." A truly loving relationship had brought liberty and expansiveness into a dependent person's life.

What we are given in friendship helps to make us what we are. Experiences in the Scriptures verify this truth.

The Bible and Friendship

Biblical persons experienced the sacred bond of friendship, linking them as closely as ties of blood. We read in 1 Samuel 23:16: "Jonathan, Saul's son, rose, and went to David at Horesh, and strengthened his hand in God." This was during a particularly perilous time when Saul sought to kill David. Men in ancient times took oaths of mutual loyalty and of common defense in a day of trouble. This helps us to understand when we read, "The soul of Jonathan was knit to the soul of David, and Jonathan loved him as his own soul" (1 Sam. 18:1). Such friends shared their dangers and fortunes without hesitation. David, armed with Jonathan's friendship, could face Saul strengthened and uplifted in heart.

The Bible distinguishes varied ministries performed between friends. That of David and Jonathan was the ministry of *companionship, understanding, trust,* and *affirmation.* An ancient wise man wrote, "A friend loves at all times, and a brother is born for adversity" (Prov. 17:17). The friendship between Ruth and Naomi, for instance, was characterized by physical *presence,* mutual *support,* and spiritual *encouragement.* Theirs was a relationship of shared sorrows, hopes, and joys.

You may recall the beautiful story from the Old Testament book of Ruth of a friendship which emerged between a Jewish woman, Naomi, and her Moabitess daughter-in-law, Ruth. Naomi and her husband, Elimelech, moved from Judah to Moab with their two sons. In time the youths married Moabite women; later all three men died. Naomi decided to return to her homeland and encouraged her daughters-in-law, Ruth and Orpah, to remain in Moab. Orpah kissed her mother-in-law farewell, but Ruth clung to her and affirmed her love.

Here is one of the most moving testimonies in all the Scriptures. "Entreat me not to leave you or to return from following you; for where you go I will go, and where you lodge I will lodge; your people shall be my people, and your God my God" (Ruth 1:16). Ruth turned her back on her people and on her gods, saying, "Where you die I will die, and there will I be buried" (Ruth 1:17). The story unfolds of her gleaning in the fields of Boaz, a close relative of Naomi. Boaz cared for Ruth and commended her fidelity to her mother-in-law: "The Lord recompense you for what you have done, and a full reward be given you by the Lord, the God of Israel, under whose wings you have come to take refuge!" (Ruth 2:12). In time, they were married; thus, a foreigner was bonded into the ancestral line of Jesus the Messiah.

Friendship was something freely chosen in biblical times. Jesus said to his disciples, "I chose you and appointed you that you should go and bear fruit" (John 15:16). Elsewhere we read, "Now Jesus loved Martha and her sister and Lazarus" (John 11:5). His friendship prompted frequent visits into their home at Bethany, mealtime fellowship, and mutually enriching

88

regard. When Lazarus became ill and died, Jesus responded with profound emotion and miraculous action by restoring him to life (John 11:1–44).

Jesus did not refer to his work associates as mere servants but rather as friends (John 15:15). We can imagine that he drew strength and encouragement from their extended association. Women as well as men "ministered unto him" in the days of his flesh, and were pictured, along with his disciples, as "beholding afar off" at the crucifixion (Matt. 27:55–56, KJV).

What would the apostle Paul have been without his friends? You may recall the difficulty he had after his conversion in convincing the believers at Jerusalem of his authentic faith. They feared Saul since he had persecuted and jailed their fellow workers. It was Barnabas, whose name means "one who encourages," who took Paul to the apostles and explained his remarkable encounter with Christ on the road to Damascus (Acts 9:27). Paul's tributes to friendship are numerous. He wrote of Priscilla and Aquila, fellow tentmakers, "who have for my life laid down their own necks: unto whom not only I give thanks, but also all the churches of the Gentiles (Rom. 16:4, KJV). To his young friend Timothy he noted, "The Lord grant mercy to the household of Onesiphorus, for he often refreshed me: he was not ashamed of my chains" (2 Tim. 1:16). On his journey to Rome, friends came in advance to meet him. "On seeing them Paul thanked God and took courage" (Acts 28:15). What a remarkable band of friends Paul discovered and developed during a lifetime of Christian service. His contribution would have been immeasurably poorer without them.

What Friendship Can Do

Friendship unlocks the doors of loneliness and opens us to the world of other people, arts, letters, history, places, and events. It permits us to walk together, rather than alone, and to share some of life's most meaningful and memorable moments.

In *The Four Loves,* the late C. S. Lewis distinguished friendship from affection and eros. "Without Eros none of us would have been begotten and without Affection none of us would have been reared; but we can live and breed without Friendship." [2] It was the exalted nature of friendship that caused its appreciation among the ancients. Affection and eros were emotions too obviously shared with lower life forms, continued Lewis. "But in Friendship—in that luminous, tranquil, rational world of relationships freely chosen—you got away from all that. This alone of all loves seemed to raise you to the level of gods or angels . . . . Friendship is a relation between men at their highest level of individuality." Think of those individuals whose input has enriched your life, the joy of discovering their uniqueness, the surprise of sharing your gifts with theirs. How diminished, how colorless life might have been without their varied contributions.

Emerson felt that friends were persons who cared about the same truth. A man of letters himself, he sensed that the magnetism of great ideas drew persons of similar persuasion together. Certainly, research projects by space, cancer, and heart surgery teams have bonded selective acquaintances into close groups of secure companions. And politicans have formed alliances in support of similar legislative programs. Yet, friendship is more than pursuit of truth, shared logic, or mutual appreciation of art, music, or ideas.

True friends break us out of narrow walls of prejudice, move us from age and health restrictions to universal concerns, and challenge us to useful creativeness. They inspire us by worthy examples and brace us in days of difficulty. Indeed, friends are often rescuers. They risk their own lives and sacrifice their fortunes so that a dear friend might have a new start. "Greater love has no man than this, that a man lay down his life for his friends" (John 15:13). These soaring words of Jesus may be illustrated in an incident from his own ministry.

Christ's fame had preceded him to the seaside community of Capernaum (see Mark 2:1–12). Crowds packed the house where he was preaching; even the door was blocked so that no other persons could enter. Four friends came carrying a crippled man whom they wished healed. Since there were no wheelchairs in that day, the paralytic was carried on a pallet with a friend at each corner. We read: "When they could not get near [Jesus] because of the crowd, they removed the roof above him; and when they had made an opening, they let down the pallet on which the paralytic lay" (Mark 2:4). What audacity!

Mark records carefully, "And when Jesus saw their faith, he said to the paralytic, 'My son, your sins are forgiven,' " (Mark 2:5). These men loaned their faith and effort to a crippled friend. It was their *faith,* not brashness, that attracted Jesus' attention. They had no idea what the Master would say or do. "Rise," he said to the paralytic, "take up your pallet and go home" (Mark 2:11). The crippled man obeyed, and the crowd was amazed, saying, "We never saw anything like this!" (Mark 2:12). Since the crowd glorified God when the man's symptoms disappeared, how much more his friends must have rejoiced. We can imagine them relating the experience to relatives and friends in later years, about pooling their care for a paralytic neighbor.

Grady Nutt has described such special ministry actions with an innovative term—"carepooling." To quote from his *Agaperos:* [3]

CAREPOOLING
  A team spirit that delights
    when no one cares
    who gets credit for success
      victory
      accomplishment . . .
CAREPOOLING
  Making the church an
    unselfish
    compassionate
    concerned

band of Samaritans
in search of
ditchdwellers . . .
CAREPOOLING
Thirstquenching
Hungersatisfying
Nakedclothing
Prisonervisiting
because we love
not
because we get credit . . .
CAREPOOLING
To *be* a cooperative program
not just vote for it . . .
CAREPOOLING
Serving and ministering
to a community
campus
nation
whether anyone joins
our group
or not . . .
CAREPOOLING
Treating God's world
God's way . . .
like a coach
not
like a referee . . .
remembering:
"God sent his Son
into the world
not to condemn the world
but that through him
the world might be saved . . ."
CAREPOOLING . . .
Caring enough
to give our very best . . .
together!

The pace and circumstances of modern life have greatly increased the fragility of friendships. This makes it discouraging to start new ones and difficult to preserve old, cherished ones. Still, deep friendships exist as the most important emotional bonds between ourselves and human beings outside our immediate families. Precisely because of our chronic job displacement, continuing changes of address, suspicion of closeness between the sexes, and competitive, success-oriented frame of mind we need friends.

One must struggle against forces nowadays that tend to undercut and destroy friendship. If companions become an extra weight on time, money, or emotions, we tend to drop them. A move often means out-of-sight-out-of-mind, with little contact between former associates. Morton M. Hunt has noted: "Even the modern bulwarks against personal disaster— Social Security, unemployment insurance, health and retirement programs—mean that a man no longer faces troubles by himself; where he once needed warm living friends, he now has cold, inhumanly efficient ones." [4] Life is all the poorer because of it. Unfortunately, closeness may breed contempt. Friendship may be abused, and former companions can come to despise or hate one another.

To Have a Friend, Be One

Since friendship is so valuable, how can we cultivate it, despite influences that tend to erode it? One, we must practice it continually, performing acts of friendship, like staying in touch, expressing appreciation, showing affection, exchanging gifts, praying for the other, rejoicing in victories, and undergirding in sorrows. We must exercise friendship as a lively process rather than view it as a finished product to take for granted. Like riding a bicycle, one must work at cultivating friends in order to claim them. Some persons think, mistakenly, that true friendship can endure, though time, distance, or silence may intervene. There may be instances to prove it, but this belief is usually an excuse for neglect and laziness. "The only way to have a friend," wrote Emerson, "is to be one."

Friendship, like good agriculture, requires cultivation; it, in turn, puts nourishment back into us. That implies effort, skill, intentionality, and planning. On our daily list of actions to be taken, for example, we ought to write it down as urgent business to visit, call, drop a note, or send a gift to a friend. How easy it is to presume upon a friendship, hoping that the individual will "understand" our preoccupation with more urgent matters.

A professional man once determined to reconstruct his daily schedule to ensure time for a leisurely luncheon visit with one friend at a time. He refused to allot this period to business conferences or to larger get-togethers. "How often," he noted, "can you feel close to an old friend or exchange your innermost thoughts with him in a roomful of company— or even in front of a third friend?"

Two, we can be open to the lifeburst of new companions, sensitive to new people in our midst and chose new friends carefully. This means reaching out to, making time for, and affirming the other person. Sometimes a couple will discover a new family moving into a neighborhood, welcome them with a visit, perhaps a gift basket of fruit, and assist them in the transition from one city to another. On the other hand, we may be chosen by a dependent single person, a struggling widow or divorcee, or someone confused in life's pressure cooker conflicts. A friendship must have meaning, both ways, in order to take root and thrive. If you simply are not up to a conversation or sociable evening with someone leaning heavily on you for support, it is best to say so rather then suffer through it. When emotionally drained, we are in need of support ourselves and possess no gift to share with a demanding or dependent individual.

Three, we can find friends again who have sparked our interest or fired our imagination in past years. My wife and I have discovered that we need to invest some time and money on trips to visit friends who live too far off for frequent meet-

ing. And they, in turn, are always welcome as honored guests
in our home. While in college, my fiancée and a lovely girl,
majoring in the same field, were companions in a home eco-
nomics cottage one semester. Later, they both married men
with military service connections. I was returning from the
war; her friend's spouse chose the Navy as a career. Though
living across the continent from one another and enduring long
periods of silence, we have reached out to that outstanding
couple again and again. Our children are all grown and married;
now we discover more time for each other than ever before.

Such experiences remind us that there are varied levels
of friendship: casual friends, occasional friends, companionate
friends, constant friends, distant friends, supportive friends,
special friends, and exclusive friends. Each of us could name
some former friends as well. There are two levels of friendship
reserved for special mention here: with God and with one's
spouse.[5]

In fashioning priorities, based upon the deepest and most
abiding values of one's life, time must be made for God and
one's spouse. Laws of the spirit are immutable. We know that
lives that last must be built on enduring foundations, not
around places, activities, or things (Luke 6:48–49). God's
friendship with man is old and his promise of presence with
us endures, "I will be with you; I will not fail you or forsake
you" (Josh. 1:5, cf. Matt. 28:19–20). God is more than a nice
person to know. His relationship with us is based on two prior
claims: creation and redemption. He is our Father because he
fashioned us in his own image for fellowship with himself.
He is our Redeemer through Jesus Christ's death and resurrection. He also empowers us for daily living through the indwell-
ing reality of his Spirit. The gift of himself, in faithfulness
and forgiveness, cements believers to God day by day.

Likewise, friendship between husbands and wives must
be worked at; it doesn't just happen. Once we begin to let
this most basic of all human friendships slip, the toll can be
enormous. The nuptial tie remains the superlative bond be-

tween individuals. Marriage does not usurp the need for close friends of both sexes; yet, it forms a unique bond. Only when two lovers are together can they open their hearts to each other. Theirs is an exclusive union, where none save God (this includes children, parents, everyone) is nearer. Friendship in marriage is forged through specific acts of intimacy, communication, touching, wisdom, sharing, and complementing one's partner. One's spouse is to know one's self—dreams, goals, struggles, secrets, and search for meaning. Their love grows through what they experience together: of bittersweet and sunburst, of pain and joy, grief and hope.

One must work on the tendency to take one's mate for granted with the passing of time. Minivacations can restore broken communication. Gift-giving can convey appreciation and affection, and should not be performed for control or gain. Meals can be delightful ways of spending hours in conversation, with music, romance, and mutual validation and support. Hearing the concerns and complaints of the other, whether real or imagined, permits unburdening of daily hurts and pressures. An affirming response or bracing challenge can startle one's mate into identifying destructive expectations, reevaluating priorities, and developing new ways of communication.

In marriage there is a time to speak and a time to listen to one's beloved. "Let not the sun go down upon your wrath" (Eph. 4:26, KJV). Disagreements are to be resolved as they happen, and not be allowed to simmer, stew, and grow toward rage or revenge.

Marriages need not sound the death knell of friendships. There is a special joy in having one's mate become the friend of his friend. Yet the meaning and power of friendship are best retained when we meet persons as individuals, not as half of a married pair. One need not drop all family members and old friends at marriage, just as promotion in one's profession need not destroy former associations. Few persons, however, have the courage, good sense, and discipline to nurture former friendships when life changes. This is especially true of couples who move, divorce, experience death, or the breakup of familiar circumstances.

There are many ways to lose good friends: through excessive dependency, harsh criticism, unrealistic expectations, failing to stay in touch, and so on. The challenge to people who care is to form some new friendships year by year and to maintain valuable relationships. True friends reach out across all ages, sexes, ethnic groupings, and status labels. And when trusted friends precede us in death we can grieve appropriately, then move on. When Tennyson's dear friend, Arthur Hallam, died in 1833, the poet devoted seventeen years to perfecting *In Memoriam*—one of the greatest tributes in the English language. You may not put life into words, like Tennyson, but you can honor friendship by sharing your words in life.

7. When a Family Needs a Friend

We have been thinking about friendship and the difference between loneliness, shutupness, and having someone to share with, to love, and enjoy. What would life be without trusted family members, neighbors, and companions who, as friends, accept and affirm us, challenge and care for us, and rejoice with and support us in all the seasons of life?

As we think here about what we can do within our own families to support each member, young and old, and to befriend other households, there are two extremes to avoid. One extreme is to do too little for those we love until it's too late. We can fail to share family events like the birth of a child, religious conversion of a youth, obtaining a driver's license, commencement from school, marriage of a fine couple, promotion at work, and achievements in later years.

Too, we can fail to share family struggles and heartaches like the diagnosis of cancer, with a long series of chemotherapy or radiation treatments to follow; a child who was sexually molested; hospitalization; separation through divorce or grief through death; and institutionalization of an aging parent.

Someone I know called to invite a friend and her husband to join a group of their favorite people at a dinner party. "I'm so glad you called," said Bobbie. "We've just experienced one of the hardest weekends of our lives. My mother, who is in her seventies, had lived with us for eight months last year. She didn't like being away from her small-town setting, church, and friends back home. She just couldn't get used to things here, with our hustle and bustle, the children's schedules, and so on. So, she went back home a few months ago. Some neigh-

bors notified us that she wasn't eating right, that she was for-
getful, and was really in danger of burning the house down
or having a serious accident."

"We brought her here this weekend and placed her in
Fireside Manor—you know, that nice retirement center out
by the lake. (Pause.) Is she ever mad at me now! I suppose
it's best that it's me and not anyone else, but this has been
one of the hardest things I've ever had to do in my whole
life. We know she'll have the best of care, good food, a limited
schedule, and medical assistance when needed. Still, we want
her to feel loved and to sense the security of our nearness if
she needs us."

Marge, the hostess caller, had aging parents who were
moving toward the close of usual life expectancy. Her husband's mother had outlived his father by many years. So she
understood Bobbie's mixed feelings of responsibility and
shame.

"You know, Bobbie," she said reassuringly, "when we
were young our parents did things for us that they thought
were best for us. We may not have agreed with their wisdom,
but they did it anyway because they thought it was best. Now,
the tables are turned. Our parents are old and dependent upon
our decisions in cases like you've mentioned. You just have
to size up the situation and do what you hope and pray is
wisest and best."

When Bobbie talked and her feelings came out scared and
ashamed, her friend reassured her. When she felt need for
clarification of emotions, Marge helped her to sort out worry
from wisdom. Because she needed approval for acting in as
responsible a manner as she knew how, her friend blessed
and affirmed her. Small wonder the telephone conversation
concluded with Bobbie's warm gratitude for someone who
cared.

Some people have been so eager to avoid the extreme of
doing too little that they have made a kind of obstacle course
out of helping friends. They are *doing* for someone all the time
to the point of neglect of their own health, their families, and

their financial and emotional resources. You may know some-one who makes a big job out of every little act of friendship, who wants more credit for caring than he deserves, or projects personal conflicts onto other people. Here's a woman, for example, who says, "I'm always trying to help and getting into trouble because of it." This is the very opposite of wise concern for others.

There are numerous occasions when feelings of isolation, loneliness, and anxiety become exaggerated. With a little help from our friends, we can obtain new insight and the strength to move ahead. But the place to begin in family ministries is with sharing occasions of joy.

Rejoice with Those Who Rejoice

Biblical writers recognized the need to claim life's good feelings as well as to share life's heartaches. The apostle Paul expressed it well: "Rejoice with those who rejoice, weep with those who weep" (Rom. 12:15). I was reared in a day when parents policed children's emotions. Around grown-ups it was unwise to make a lot of noise, with either sounds of happiness or sadness. Children celebrating at my grandparents' house were bridled like wild, young horses. If things got too hilarious or out of hand, a warning came from the kitchen: "Now, children, play pretty" (which, being interpreted, meant: "Get quiet; you are being too noisy!").

The opposite was also true. After punishment for some "crime," like arguing with my sister, I was warned to "dry right up!" which meant NO TEARS ALLOWED. At funerals the folks in my Southern community were stoical. We sat on our feelings; too many tears were an evidence of a weak faith. The ideal person was the one who always remained calm and controlled. Neither parties nor pressures were to ruffle us too much. I still have a poem my mother clipped and shared with me as a youth: "Life is mostly froth and bubbles. Only two things stand like stone: kindness in another's troubles, courage in your own."

There is wisdom in leading with one's head rather than

one's heart in life's encounters. On the other hand, life scripts (in Transactional Analysis terms) do include the *child* part of personality, along with *parent* and *adult* aspects. We need the freedom of little children, as Jesus himself said, in order to inherit God's blessing (Matt. 18:3). By that I mean the spontaneous honesty, genuine humility, and lack of subtle duplicity of children. They cry and laugh without restraint and permit others to do the same.

Rejoicing with those who rejoice implies seeing the bright and beautiful, not just the dark, aspects of experience. Joy builds on the other person's strengths; it does not "pull the plug" on one's neighbor or put him down time and again. An executive was making a new start, for example, through personal conferences with employees. "One thing I've learned to appreciate about you is your fine sense of humor," said one man. "Without humor we could not live," came the rejoinder.

We can rejoice at the wedding reception of a young couple and at the birth of their children. Here, for example, is a letter I wrote to a newborn, the first child of a dear friend, as a way of congratulating her parents and welcoming her into the world.

Dear Jennifer:

It may be some time before we are able to meet personally. Therefore, I am writing to tell you how happy Gloria and I are about your safe arrival on Planet Earth. A little girl is the freshest thing I know from the hands of God, and he has been so good to give you to your mother and daddy.

January 31, your birth date, will be special for me since my birthday is the 15th of January each year.

Entering this world is a pretty big job, so you might have to work and wiggle your way into people's lives. Some folks will try to make it easy for you, especially your wonderful parents. They are two fantastic people. You will get to know them real well in the months and years ahead.

I thank our Heavenly Father for your safe arrival and ask his blessings upon you at each stage of your growth. Jennifer Smith will be special for me wherever you are for as long as you live. God bless you.

Your new friend,

Were you to prefer to address the letter to the parents, rather than offer an entry for the baby's memory book, a letter could be worded like this.

Dear Roy and Candy:

Warmest congratulations upon the safe arrival of your son, James Warren, March 15. Am so glad to know that he is here safely. Trust that Candy is doing nicely and that both of you are becoming accustomed to God's fresh gift in your lives.

It is always good to hear from you and to know of the splendid work that you are doing.

Yours in friendship,

Enrolling for driver's education class is one of the biggest steps a young person takes on the way to adulthood in Western culture. After weeks of classroom instruction, the students move to a driver's track, city streets, busy freeways, and multi-lane turnpikes. Why not rejoice with teenagers when they pass all tests with flying colors and obtain a driver's license? To one such young woman I sent the following note.

Dear Debbie:

Congratulations!

During a conversation that your father and I had today he told me that you have just celebrated your sixteenth birthday anniversary and have obtained your driver's license. Those are both big events in a lovely young lady's life. And I applaud your achievements.

It is a joy to see you growing up so beautifully in our midst. Count on my friendship and appreciation for you.

Most sincerely,

I recall the time a gift certificate came through the mail as a friend, in a distant city, reached across the miles and remembered my birthday. It melted me. What a nice surprise it was to have his birthday greetings in the day's mail, along with authorization to purchase a book from the campus store. Another memorable event was the housewarming of our new lake home. Gloria had prepared her famous Louisiana gumbo and hot plum cake for about twenty guests. We had sent invitations and maps directing people to our new retreat cottage. Friends responded with lovely gifts, a meal together, and a memorable evening of table games and enjoyable conversation.

When people have walked the "second mile" with us, we can share our gratitude, whatever the occasion. When hospitality has been given, on an overnight stay or a special meal, a "thank-you" note is in order. Congratulations may be sent to one obtaining a new job or someone promoted in rank. A friend elected to a prominent post in denominational life should know of our joy and receive our congratulations.

Such rejoicing is what Myron and Mary Ben Madden, in *The Time of Your Life,* call "claiming the good feelings." They suggest that joy, peace, and hope lie at the center of positivity. "Joy is the child in the person," state the Maddens. "Peace is the assurance that what is, is all right, and that what comes will be all right, too . . . . Hope is the power of the future to shape the present." [1] Such optimistic states, they caution, do not avoid the shadow side of existence. We still must board up our windows, nail down our shutters, and store provisions against the storm. Rejoicing is possible, however, as one determines that no matter how many times he is engulfed, he can take the pieces left and start life over.

Helping with Life's Transitions

Life moves; life changes. Like the restless sea, we are always in motion—in both the silent depths of profound mysterious experiences and the sparkling, sunny shallows which splash on the shore. Transitions come in the normal passing of time. One is soon beyond the lighthearted years of school—harnessed into the world of work, competition, success, and survival. Aging begins at birth and continues until the last breath is drawn in our human frame. Stages can be identified—like childhood, youth, adulthood, and old age—each of which has its unique requirements for growth.

The late Lewis Sherrill saw these stages shaped into *The Struggle of the Soul;* Alex Haley traced his family saga through two centuries as *Roots;* and investigative reporter Gail Sheehy called maturation tasks *Passages: Predictable Crises of Adult Life.* [2] John R. Claypool addressed human development sermonically as "the art of living the expected." He noted four great *Stages* with accompanying tasks of learning and living: (1) Childhood—the need to be anointed with delight by one's parents; (2) Adolescence—the need to negotiate life's valley of transition; (3) Adulthood—the need to travel up and down life's mountain; and (4) Senior Adulthood—the need to focus on being. [3] Such transitions are more than mere stages, however; they form the great evaluation periods of existence. One needs not merely the experience of living through the stages but skill in making sense out of them and wisdom to find polar stars for guidance through them.

It is not only we who age, but history itself shifts. Life squeezes us in its grip, tests us with its fate, or implores us to move ahead with courage. Reporter Russell Baker of *The New York Times* has noted that the "good life" is dying in America. The meaning of seventy-cent-a-gallon gasoline, $250 electricity bills, and 10 percent mortgages is that the good life is over, dead. The good life was born in the autumn of 1945 and died in a gasoline line in the mid-1970s. This is no longer the land of plenty, where there is more and more of everything—sex, gold, forests, energy, youth, and so on. We have lived into a time of limited resources, meat substitutes like soy by-products, 2,800 pound automobiles, 55-mile-per-hour interstate speed, and cautiously (rather than climate) controlled air conditioning in our homes, cars, school rooms, and offices.

Change is our constant companion. Our children were reared on real meat hamburgers, while watching Ding Dong

School, and Mother and Daddy were convinced that getting what they went after in life was really possible. The home, ideally, was thought to be as solid as the Rock of Gibraltar. Now, we wonder if someone has moved that British colony because change rather than certainty is the order of the day. Art, popular music, books, and films form a fleeting commentary on our fragmented lives. Hit musical groups spin into and out of fashion as rapidly as their pop records spin on radio studios' turntables.

Sooner or later, the good life does die, one way or another, for all of us. Everything that has worked for us in the past does not always work for us in the present or may not work perfectly in the future. To confess our hurt, to admit times when we have missed the boat, and to reveal the need for help that each one of us has should solidify us rather than separate us from fellow human beings. We really do share in the universality of sin and suffering and hurt and need.

A church fellowship is to "do good to all men, and especially to those who are of the household of faith" (Gal. 6:10). That is the ideal. I think too often that theologians, church leaders, and laypersons who are supposed to care are not always sensitive to people's needs. We, who are naturally self-seeking, do not do good to all members of the household of faith. Too often our love is on paper not in what we do. Our caring is what we talk about or remember from the past, rather than some action we take. So it heartens me when I learn of a church fellowship that actually is alive and caring.

How might one help when a family moves into one's neighborhood or a new employee joins one's staff? The "hello" call is so easy to make, just a brief introductory visit to welcome the new family and to assure them of goodwill. Supplying names of physicians, dentists, reliable retail outlets, and so on can help new arrivals to negotiate the tricky maze of a different city. Adding money to time (it costs to care), one could take a bouquet of flowers, potted plant, jar of homemade jelly, or basket of fruit, along with a note of genuine warmth.

Inviting a new resident to one's Sunday School class or to worship at one's church helps both the family and the congregation.

Retirement may be one of the toughest transitions of all. In addition to the company party and traditional gift of an inscribed watch, is there anything a friend can do for someone who has reached retirement age? A meal with the couple cements friendship, and remembering them after the party is over is urgent. A letter may also be encouraging. Consider the text of a note I sent to a fellow teacher who retired, and whose wife, a public-school teacher, joined him for years of leisure.

Dear Bill and Mildred:

You are two of the people who have meant the most to Gloria and me in the quarter century that we have been associated with Southwestern Baptist Theological Seminary. This week as Bill completed the cleaning out of his office and turned his keys over to a new occupant, I have reflected upon the richness of our relationships through the years. This is just a note to say how much we have enjoyed you, how much we appreciate you now, and that Gloria and I will continue to covet and cherish your friendship which is one of the dearest possessions of our lives.

Bill, thank you for your example of devotion to God, quiet dignity, delightful humor, disciplined scholarship, and comradely care. The enclosed publication may be one that you have seen before but may be not. I commend the American Association of Retired Persons to you, *Modern Maturity* magazine, and all the resources that "Senior Power" represents. Thanks for your prayers in our behalf through the years, your words of encouragement, the delicious meals in your home, and the times of games, fun, and fellowship.

As I said to you this week, Bill, the door of the faculty room is always open in the School of Theology. And you are our friend. So, while weaning is a part of leave-taking, there is a sense in which we need you as much or more than you need us. So visit "the Hill" often. Meanwhile, have a wonderful summer, and let's keep in touch for fellowship and recreation.

                                    With warmest regards,

Retirement is a maturational crisis that we each face. Through aging we will be challenged by similar adventures and adversities that affect other persons. Even as we speak in New Testament terms of "the strong bearing the burdens of the weak," we recognize that the strong sometimes become weak and the weak become strong. Roles may be reversed. In time, the growing child will minister to the grown-up, even as the adult now ministers to his children.

Journalist Russell Baker reported that the "good life" is dying in the United States. Need that be so for God's persons? In actual fact, *the* good life is born again and again through what Christian people care about, trust, invest in, nurture, and love. Such care is not just a burden or pious sentimentality. Care is more than a feeling; it goes to great efforts to reach out and touch, wish someone well, resolve a grievance, or help in adversity. Care is more than wishing; it is hoping for the best and working toward justice for all people everywhere.

Weep with Those Who Weep

We've looked at happy occasions in family life and examined care in normal transitions from birth to old age. What can be done when the hard, difficult times come? I'll try to answer that question, illustrating it in four areas. What can be done when a child rebels or is arrested? What can be done in marriage conflict? What can be done when a child is born with birth defects? What can be done when mental illness strikes?

Officials of the National Council on Crime and Delinquency remind us that 90 percent of American young people, aged 13–16, commit crimes for which they might be arrested if they were caught. If a person is caught, he needs legal advice or counsel. There are things for parents and friends to avoid and certain helpful things to practice. If a child is arrested, the parent should not join the police in questioning the child. They should not attack the police and say, "You framed our child." A parent should not threaten a child in police headquarters with words like, "Just wait until I get you home because I am going to take you apart." The police would probably want to keep the child in jail for safety if they sense that the parents are going to brutalize him.

To help one under arrest, first obtain legal aid. Someone facing indictment must know his rights and responsibilities under the law. Such a youth needs support, understanding, confrontation with his need for confession, forgiveness, and an opportunity, if possible, to make restitution. If delinquents cannot actually repay for the damage they have done, parents ought to arrange some symbolic way in which restitution can be made (work, with or without pay, or the like).

An angry teenage boy once set fire to the offices of his high school. Before the fire department was able to extinguish the fire, major damage had been done. His father begged police to let him be indicted, stand trial, and face sentencing instead of his son. The offer was refused, and a juvenile rehabilitation program was arranged. The son did not escape imprisonment, but he learned new aspects of his Christian father's love for him. In time, he was convinced of his heavenly Father's forgiveness as well.

What can be done for someone experiencing marriage conflict? For one thing, we can recognize that it's too easy to get married in most states. It is harder to get an automobile license or a fishing or hunting license than a marriage license in many counties. A license doesn't cost much. It's also too easy to get unmarried. In 1970, California moved toward no fault divorce and changed the legal proceeding to dissolution, not divorce. The old adversary system was dropped. Yet, in that same year, there were more than 100,000 dissolutions of marriage in the state of California.

According to the United States Census Bureau, our divorce rate has climbed to more than one million a year. Homosexuals, now "out of the closet," seek legitimation of their alternative living arrangements and full civil rights. Each numeral in a statistical report represents a human being with needs.

Again we realize that there are complex factors, personal, cultural, and situational, leading to marriage conflict. Personal factors underlying crises include variables like one's self-concept, religious, and value differences, degree of maturity, ability to manage money, sexual behavior, vocational identity, willingness to work, commitment to or infidelity in the marriage, health, alcohol, and drug abuse, and the like. Their resolution may require months of hard work in counseling plus the desire and determination to make the marriage work.

Situational factors must also be examined and resolved. Some changes outside the nuclear family, like war or a depression, exert incredible pressure on couples. Changes in families of origin, like a grandparent's illness or a father's job loss, induce stress. Financial matters can shift and resentments run high between couples and families of origin. Changes within the nuclear group, like the birth of another child or receiving a parental resident into the family circle, can cause disequilibrium. Biological changes provoke stress, as when a mother reaches menopause or a father is injured or suffers a stroke. Social changes, like a husband's dismissal from his job or a child's departure for school or military service, depress family members.

Complexity of conflict is intensified with the passing of time. The longer problems of relationship persist the harder it is to reverse the process and see a couple move toward health. The best thing family members and friends can do is to intervene when the conflicts are still minor or manageable. Hearing the blame, self-doubt, projection of anger, and confusion of a helpee can be trying. It might require the service of a qualified pastoral counselor or psychiatrist.

Some couples give up on marriage and go their own way. If the family cannot be saved and the marriage is dead, one's goal should be to save the personalities involved.[4] Divorce is never an ideal because it misses God's original intent. Marriage was not to be dissolved, save by death, in his plan (Matt. 19:3–12). Still, divorce is not the unpardonable sin. There has to be a way of making room for persons who have missed the mark. They must work through their anger, sense of failure, sorrow, and social isolation to a sense of forgiveness. We need to restore formerly married persons to fellowship within the Christian community.

The third issue is, What if a home receives into its membership a birth defective child? More than one percent of all infants are born with congenital handicaps of a physical or mental nature or both. We can only imagine the effect on the whole family when a child arrives with a severe birth defect.[5] Parents of special children sometimes tend to feel that God is evening the score with them for something that they have done or have failed to do. There is no sorrow like the chronic sorrow of a person with a defective child because the grief does not go away.

A young man spoke of his sister, "She is now thirty-one years of age. The doctors told my mother and dad that she would die before she was five years old. She has lived twenty-six years beyond that." He was appealing to a group of young ministers, "Be tender when you come to this kind of task."

Some parents will shop around endlessly for a physician to tell them that their child will grow out of a certain condition, like mongoloidism, a heart anomaly, or cerebral palsy. Some parents of mentally retarded children have become victims of charlatans. Some will "forget" what a doctor has said about the child's limitations. Others fret endlessly over whether to place the child in a specialized institution. They will resist a pessimistic medical diagnosis. They will refuse to accept the regimen and schedules of medication that some physicians might impose.

Certain parents of special children feel rejected by heaven. Thus they become angry with God or they become angry with people who have normal children. They may become impatient with the child or reject him at a deep spiritual and emotional level, while publicly trying to accept him.

T. B. Maston, who influenced generations of students at

Southwestern Baptist Theological Seminary, dedicated a small book on suffering to his multiple handicapped son, Tom Mc.[6] He and Mrs. Maston discovered early that Tom Mc had been seriously injured at birth. They took him to many doctors and several hospitals in search of help. Their hearts were saddened as doctor after doctor said: "We do not know anything that can be done for him. All you can do is take him home and give him the best possible care." And they have done that for more than half a century. The Mastons are convinced that God speaks through suffering. They have discovered some profound spiritual gifts through suffering: understanding, obedience, patience, high values, a sense of need or humility, deepened fellowship with God, a capacity to wait for him and to pray "nevertheless," while placing their lives into God's hands.

Special parents of special children need a sense of affirmation of their worth, full acceptance, and encouragement to live in Christian hope. There is a need for patient endurance, skilled medical care, financial help, and a faith to face the mystery of life without having all the answers.

One other need should be examined as we think of ministering to families. What can we do when mental illness strikes, as it does in the lives of one out of ten Americans? Emotional illness is no respecter of persons. It leaves anger, pain, hurt, and questions in its wake.

Karl Menninger and psychiatrists who have studied with him for a generation have helped to move mental health professionals away from simple classifications in diagnostic categories. Rather than labels, said Menninger in *The Vital Balance*, we should see a person with emotional illness as one who is fundamentally disturbed in relationships. Their loves have become confused. Disorders in thinking, feeling, and willing go together. Physical causes, like thyroid imbalance, also lie at the base of numerous emotional disorders.

In theological terms, the person who is locked into some kind of disorder, like a chronic depression or deep psychosis, faces a demonic struggle. A part process of experience may be elevated to first place in one's life. A young woman, for example, who feels dominated by her mother may alienate herself in hostility from the family. By denial of positive forces and self-elevation, with perfectionistic demands upon herself, such a woman becomes the center of her values. Narcissism, an unhealthy self-worship, can become the core and criterion of all her relationships. She is right in her own thoughts; everyone else is wrong. "They" (even God) are out to get her. In biblical terms, this is idolatry. One's frustration becomes one's god.

When faced with such vexing problems, Jesus Christ noted the difficulty of full cure. He confessed concerning an epileptic youth, "This kind [of possession] cannot be driven out by anything but prayer" (Mark 9:29). Complete cure may or may not come, but help is available. There is help in careful diagnosis, medication like chemotherapy, counseling, play or work therapy, sometimes from the care that comes with temporary hospitalization.[7]

What is the word for us in these disorders and in all of the growing edges noted in this discussion? The word is *care*—wise, strong, yet tender concern. Some instances of need can be met in our day to day rounds of living. Others, with complex symptoms and exhausting demands, require the finest medical assistance available. Getting such help does not deny God's care; rather, it is a profound act of faith.

8 How to Help in a Crisis

In chapter 7 we saw how life's normal transitions, from birth to death, offer various opportunities for helping. An individual in her sixties, for example, may have passed successfully through all life stages to date: from her own childhood to adolescence, puberty to marriage, birth of her first child to the last child's departure from home, from middle to senior adulthood, and so on. Suddenly, at age sixty-nine, the woman developed physical sympoms: dizziness, elevated blood pressure, excessively rapid heart rate, and weakness.

She had been hospitalized in past years for several major surgical procedures. Yet, all her vital organic systems had functioned reliably before. She had moved along from year to year, meeting the problems and challenges of life in a more or less efficient way. This new heart complication was so novel and threatening, however, that her usual ways of coping with health concerns no longer worked. She experienced severe headaches, anxiety upon being hospitalized by her cardiologist, increased dependency upon family and friends, loss of self-esteem, and decreased efficiency after returning home.

Her normal developmental stages gave way to a threatening situational crisis. The word *crisis* implies a critical turning point or boundary situation, during which things could become better or worse. In illness a crisis implies a life or death period when a patient's condition might improve or deteriorate. Intensive care is indicated, and every resource that medical science can muster is employed. Often, the doctor says to family members, "We've done everything we know to do. For the next twenty-four to thirty-six hours we must pray and hope for the best." From an individual perspective, a crisis is any event or set of circumstances which threatens a person's sense of well-being and interferes with his usual routine.

When families were larger and members lived close by, relatives depended upon each other to help when crises arose. Here is an instance of a family whose house, located in a rural area, burned to the ground. The occupant's brother-in-law literally took off from work and built a new residence on the spot where the former cottage had stood. Because of the occupant's poverty and his brother-in-law's generosity, the new house was provided at no cost. It was a gift which, unfortunately, the original owner failed to appreciate. Thanklessness is part of the risk which helpers take, as Jesus disclosed after healing ten lepers (Luke 17:17).

Because nuclear families (husbands, wives, and children) have moved away from their extended family roots, people have had to discover other helpers. When trouble comes or illness strikes we turn to neighbors, friends, fellow church members, and ministers. These are the people near at hand, who are dearest to us and best able to help.

When Folks Cry Help!

I have implied that there are two major kinds of crises in human experience—normal *developmental* concerns which occur in the maturational process and *situational* crises which occur in times of accident, disruption, illness, or death. Here is a young wife, whom we shall call Ann, who is the mother of two children. Ann works outside the home as a co-provider with her husband. One Sunday night, she showed up suddenly at her parents' home, upset and crying. Ann didn't say exactly what was wrong but indicated that she and Jim (her husband) had had a big fuss.

In the course of Ann's conversation with her parents, she began to cry hysterically. They did not know what to do for her. In all of her thirty-three years of normal development, Ann had never fallen apart like that. Near midnight, her father called a minister friend and asked his advice. "What can we do for her?" he implored, after explaining the circumstances. His pastor suggested that they take Ann to the emergency room of a nearby hospital, see a physician, request sedation, and seek temporary admission. He had seen cases of hysteria before and felt that her uncontrollable crying would pass.

Along with her family, the minister sensed that Ann was beyond the boundaries of normal coping. In this unique situation, she needed a medical appraisal, protective care, and eventually an opportunity for counseling.

We might wonder what had happened between Ann and Jim that night that caused her to withdraw in dependency to her parents' home. They may have failed to go to church that day, as on many other Sundays, and may have been trying to resolve differences about religion. Jim may have been out on a hunting trip with his friends that weekend; Ann and the children may have felt abandoned. He may have been drinking and said some things which Ann resented. Jim may have become forceful, even violent, in a trial-and-error attempt to obtain sex. In the tension, frustration, and confusion (whatever the circumstances), their differences burst into uncontrollable emotions. Ann got out of the house before something worse might have happened.

When crises come all of one's inner resouces are mobilized. Ann drew on all her reserves of physical strength, patience, devotion, and familiar methods of response. Sensing that the circumstances might become worse or, at least, were not going to change, and exhausting her known ways of coping, Ann collapsed. Later, one caught in such a trap might recall what has gone on before, with feelings of anger, rejection, frustration, and failure. Such demoralization often precedes a so-called nervous breakdown. There is no more stamina left to deal with the stress, so the person withdraws from reality or persists irrationally in some behavior which denies the problem but does nothing to solve it.

No two people react to crucial situations in the same way.

Each crisis time is unique in our lives. Reactions depend upon one's flexibility and courage, novelty in coping or adaptation to stress, ego strength or sense of worth, spiritual resources or walk with God, one's past experiences or patterns of coping, and one's outlook of hopeful optimism ("Things will work out") or dreary pessimism ("I'll never make it"). One thing for certain, a time of crisis for a person or family is socially isolating, emotionally debilitating, physically exhausting, and financially draining.

One woman put it this way: "I was not just at the end of my rope. I was barely hanging on to the knot at the end, swinging over a cliff and about to let go. I do not know what I would have done if Cindy (a nurse friend) had not come when she did."

The availability of people who can help makes a tremendous difference in someone's reaction to a crisis. It is difficult to predict what any individual, including ourselves, might do in a specific set of circumstances. Given a diagnosis of cancer, for example, one person might react in smoldering anger with God; another might give up in resignation to fate; while a third individual might draw upon spiritual reserves in coping with prolonged periods of pain. People who care need to know what to expect as crises develop, as well as how to help victims cope.

What to Expect

Perhaps the best response to someone's question, What shall we expect or look for? is this: Expect the unexpected. Researchers in the field of crisis counseling have discovered some common characteristics of people who call for help.[1]

There is some *anxiety* which causes a person or his family to use poor judgment in seeking a resolution to the problem. Someone who has lost his assets through gambling, for example, may borrow more money at an exorbitant interest rate, which adds to the problems. Often there is a sense of *helplessness*. We read of persons in public life who become drug or alcohol dependent. They may be institutionalized under a fake diagnosis but actually receive group therapy, diet control, and medical guidance to get unhooked. An alcoholic wife of a prominent politician, for example, may not know what to do. She feels ashamed because she is not self-reliant and too conspicuous to admit need. A crisis, like an overdose of pills or an automobile accident when intoxicated, becomes a cry for help.

A *dependence on others* is often inevitable and can create other problems. When someone is down he can resent it. His anger can be turned inward in depression, outward in rage toward family or associates, or upward in rejection of God. When trouble comes a person may shrink in despair or rely upon helpers to see him through. Helplessness, however, contributes to *loss of self-esteem* because the person has lost control of life and feels victimized by fate. A man driving a truck for twenty years accidentally pinned his arm between a vehicle he was unloading and the frame of his automobile transport trailer. He could never work again. In one inattentive moment an accident, which might have been prevented, cut off his arm, his income, and his future. As an amputee, every action of his life was altered.

Anger over the whole situation is a common emotion. It is sometimes hidden but often aimed at people nearby who are trying to help. The man's wife, in the above instance, could not understand his bouts of depression and self-pity at first. When he lashed out at her, she felt rejected and became angry in reaction herself. His anger was also aimed at God, with the remaining good fist doubled up in heaven's face. Resentment was compounded with guilt for failing to cope effectively with his loss and forced retirement. One calling on such a patient in the hospital or, later, at home needs to understand that such anger is not directed at him but at life. In time, a sufferer should work through grief and anger, accept his new body image, and move ahead with life.

Crises are more than minor upsets in one's daily routine. After a blow, one's attention suddenly focuses inward. He is fighting for his health, status, place, sanity, his very existence.

There is *decreasing efficiency* in one's daily output. One spends much time in worrying about why "something like this has happened to me." He frets, prays, ruminates on the problem, recalls what went wrong, perhaps questions God's goodness. If he has been victimized by another, as in a robbery attempt, he may wish revenge for his hurt or at least an explanation for what happened. Such wonder and worry sap time, energy, and attention which normally would be directed to efficient living.

Helping Oneself to Cope

Several questions naturally emerge in a discussion like this. One, what would I do if I were the person in trouble? Are there unhealthy things to avoid in such circumstances? Do we have any guidance for healthy coping in crisis times? How can I be serviceable to others when trouble comes? Let's address them in order.[2]

Here are some unhealthy ways to meet a crisis:
1. Deny that a problem exists
2. Evade the problem (via alcohol, for example)
3. Refuse to seek help or to accept help
4. Hide the fact that you have feelings of sorrow, anger, guilt, and so forth
5. Don't think through the nature of the crisis situation
6. Give no thought to practical ways in which you might deal with the crisis
7. Blame others for causing the crisis and expect that somebody else is totally responsible for curing it
8. Turn away from friends or family
9. Refuse to pray about the crisis
10. Convince yourself that your trouble is evidence of God's punishment or disfavor.

On the other hand, *here are healthy ways to meet a crisis:*
1. Face the fact that there is a problem
2. Attempt to understand the situation more fully

3. Open channels of communication with friends, relatives, pastors, or others who might be able to help you

4. Face up to your negative feelings of guilt, anxiety, or resentment, and consider actions and alternative ways of viewing the situation so that you can deal with these feelings

5. Separate the changeable from the unchangeable in the situation and accept that which cannot be changed

6. Explore practical ways of coping with the problem, and take steps (however small) in handling the problem in a practical way

7. Accept responsibility for coping with problems, even problems which seem to have arisen from situations beyond your control

8. Draw closer to friends and family, especially to those who are trying to be helpful

9. Pray about the matter, honestly sharing your concerns with God

10. Remember the providence of God, who loves all mankind and is both aware of our needs and concerned about us.

One of the most common forms of human coping is denial. Unpleasant and painful feelings are simply set aside. The willingness of someone to deny, deceive, even lie to oneself and others about circumstances is portrayed poignantly by novelist Eudora Welty in *The Optimist's Daughter*.[3] It is the story of Judge McKelva, his second wife Fay, and his widowed daughter, Laurel McKelva Hand, whose husband was killed in World War II. Fay Chisom McKelva, a harsh woman, was unkind to the Judge following serious eye surgery in New Orleans. She physically abused him as a patient, and thereby provoked his premature death.

After the Judge's funeral, Laurel confronted her stepmother.

"Fay, I wanted to ask you something," Laurel said. "What made you tell me what you did about your family? The time we talked, in the Hibiscus."

"What did I say?" Fay challenged her.

"You said you had nobody—no family. You lied about your family."

"If I did, that's what everybody else does," said Fay. "Why shouldn't I?"

"Not lie that they're dead."

"It's better than some lies I've heard around here!" cried Fay. She struggled to lift her suitcase, and Laurel, as if she'd just seen her in the deepest trouble, moved instinctively to help her. But Fay pushed on past her, dragging it, and hobbled in front of her, bumping her load a step ahead of her down the stairs.

Later, as Laurel poured over her late mother's belongings, she realized that it was not punishment she wanted for Fay. She desired acknowledgment from her—admission that she knew what she had done. Welty writes tellingly: "Fay, she knew now, knew beyond question, would answer, 'I don't even know what you're talking about.' This would be a fact. Fay had never dreamed that in that shattered moment in the hospital she had not been just as she always saw herself—in the right. Justified."

This experience from literature reminds us that some people are extremely hard to love. Fay had shaken her aged husband following delicate surgery; he had died soon thereafter. She denied her guilt in his death, just as she denied that she had relatives living in another state. This points up the self-justifying tendency of human nature. When we are implicated in complex situations, we seek absolution and claim a clean bill of health for ourselves. We not only want what we deserve; we want more than we merit, even at others' expense. By denying that a problem existed, hiding her shame and sorrow, and refusing to seek help, Fay McKelva faced widowhood alone.

Crisis Intervention

The unanswered question becomes, How can I help a person or family, as a positive Christian witness, when trouble comes? It is clear that family members, friends, and fellow church members form a first line of defense in crisis intervention. The closer we are to the crisis situation the more likely we are to be called on for help or to intervene by offering to help. The lay helper will be available, we learned in chapter 5, will risk involvement, and will communicate concern through flexible counseling methods.

First, we must distinguish among varied cries for help. Some cries for help emerge within the human life cycle. Developmental or maturational crises come with the tasks of growing up and older: the birth of a child, entering a child into private or public school, facing adolescent trials with a searching teenager, a child's leaving home, entering marriage, problems of aging, death, and experiences with grief.

Some cries for help are heard when trouble comes. These instances are situational and may become destructive or, at least, debilitating periods. Such crises occur like combat fatigue in the midst of life—sometimes when illness hits, a move is ordered by one's company, a promotion is accepted, a job is lost, an accident or fatal disease (like cancer) touches a loved one, and when someone we know obtains a divorce or attempts suicide.

Part of the befriender's quandary is that his "left hand does not know what his right hand is doing" in sharing stressful events with people. Just getting an anxious, talkative person off the phone or out of one's office oversimplifies the helping process. Getting rid of callers should not be equated with understanding and helping them.

The pastor's task in crises, like an accident in which several young people or members of a family are killed, is to stabilize his entire congregation. The whole church may be in shock. Denying grave tragedies or rationalizing with pious phrases about "God's will" must be avoided. A minister counsels quickly to maintain good spiritual health and to prevent serious emotional disorganization in his church family. The experienced pastor knows that, just as one bad apple spoils the entire barrel, so a deeply disturbed individual can create much havoc unless he is confronted during a crucial situation.

The first task is to determine whether a crisis actually exists. David Switzer poses three questions (in *The Minister as Crisis Counselor*) which assist with assessment.[4] When the helper can answer yes to all three questions, a crisis likely exists. One, has there been a recent (within a few weeks) onset of the troublesome feelings and/or behavior? Two, have they tended to grow progressively worse? Three, can the time of the onset be linked with some external event, some change in the person's life situation? A yes response to these questions calls for crisis intervention.

There is no standard formula or rule of thumb approach for helping people in crises. There are some things, however, which have been found useful in almost every case.

1. Given the fact that a crisis situation calls for help, one should make contact with the helpee.

Assistance provided to suicidal persons by lay befrienders in Suicide Prevention Centers (like one in Los Angeles, reported by N. L. Farberow and E. S. Schneidman in *The Cry for Help*), has encouraged volunteers to train for crisis intervention counseling.

The model of microcounseling offered here is my own adaptation of the "ABC" method which was first proposed by Warren L. Jones, a Los Angeles psychiatrist.[5] In teaching crisis counseling techniques to laypersons—volunteer workers at the Pasadena Mental Health Center—Jones developed an outline for managing each situation:

A—Achieve contact with the helpee.

B—Boil down the problem to its essentials.

C—Assist the person to cope actively through an inventory of his resources. I have added a fourth element for Christian helpers: Depend upon God for specific help in each crucial situation. Let's examine these suggestions in brief detail.

There are four chief ways to achieve contact with persons in a crisis: (1) the person is self-referred, that is he comes on his own initiative; (2) the person is referred by someone else—a family member, a physician, friend, and so on; (3) the helper initiates the relationship via a phone call, letter, or personal visit; and (4) the helper may be requested to contact an individual or family by another person.

Achieving contact has some specific goals in mind.

1. Contact with another person breaks the cycle of loneliness or sense of isolation that often accompanies a crisis. We can see Jesus Christ, after the resurrection, for example, walking with two bereaved men on the road to Emmaus. That contact made a great difference in their lives when they realized that they had been with the risen Lord (Luke 24:13–36).

2. Contact befriends the person by structuring time for a conversation and offering realistic hope within the situation.

3. Contact supports the person or family while they get facts and feelings sorted out.

4. Contact reduces panic and possible feelings of self-destructiveness. It drains off the poisons of potentially dangerous situations and affirms the worth of each individual involved. Thereby they gain new courage to live.

5. Contact encourages rest, prayer, seeking God's guidance, and recourse to viable alternatives. Such help does not deny reality. Rather, it "strengthens the person's hand in God" when he has been wounded by a tragic blow or loss.

6. Contact helps to reduce anxiety by permitting persons to talk out their fears, griefs, and confusion, and to decide upon some desirable course of action.

2. Deal with the basic issues at hand.

One may detect crisis piled on top of crisis in a single situation. This is why Warren Jones suggested simplifying the situation by focusing on essentials.

The usual response to stressful situations is mobilizing one's emotional defenses, calling on available resources, formulating strategies, and regaining one's equilibrium. On the other hand, one's feelings may give way to an anxiety state if the event is a mountain too high to climb, if adequate resources are not available, and if one's customary coping mechanisms fail to restore life's vital balance.

A minister I know was visited by a young professional man who came unexpectedly to his office. The Reverend Roger Grayford had not seen Wilfred Greene for about two years, so he was surprised to see him.

Grayford: How nice to see you! This is a pleasant surprise. How are you?

Greene: All right, I guess. (*The response was low-keyed, almost hesitant.*)

Grayford: What brings you this way today?

Greene: I've got to have some professional help. (*He explained that he was not sleeping more than a couple of hours each night.*) I can't work. I go to my desk, get preoccupied, return to my room, and try to rest. Then I go back to work.

Grayford: (*Recognizing the symptoms of depression, he asked:*) Are you on medication to help right now?

Greene: I'm taking Elavil, but I've got to have more help than that. (*They explored the matter of whether he was capable of or had thought about suicide. Taking his own life had crossed his mind; yet, he did not wish to escape from life.*)

The minister checked details of the support community available to the young man. He discovered that Greene's wife was out of the state with her parents. He had depended upon her encouragement, prodding, and affection. Now that they were separated, his situational support had evaporated.

Grayford focused on basic issues, like Greene's perception of his feelings (such as his interpretation of his crisis condition), available support community, and his coping ability.

Grayford: Can you make it with this visit or do you want the professional help mentioned earlier?

Greene: (*The reply was instantaneous.*) I think I need to see a psychiatrist. (*All of the classic symptoms of depression were there—stooped posture, low self-esteem, blend of past problems and present pressures,*

loss of appetite, sleepless nights, and ineffective functioning at work.)
It's a mountain too high for me to climb. I need help. I
need it now. (*Notice the helper's next step.*)

3. Assist the person to cope with a plan of action.

An appointment was arranged and Greene saw a physician
who specialized in emotional disorders the following day.
Medication was prescribed and a treatment program in a hospital setting was suggested. Consulting a reliable physician makes
sense in depression, particularly one that hangs on and renders
a person helpless. Therapies of choice range from somatic aids
(like electroconvulsive shock and antidepressant drugs, where
no insight is required into causes); to brief counseling, where
one's anger, ambivalence, or grief may be spilled and symptoms
relieved; to long-term psychotherapy. Usually, when relief
comes, a person does not feel much need for a radical personality change. Altering environmental circumstances may be essential—like living arrangements, work associates, and so on.
The possibility of suicide must always be considered, making
medical consultation and sometimes hospitalization essential.

We help such an individal cope through an inventory of
his perceptions of need, resources, and plans for action. How
does the person perceive the event—as one internal to his present condition or externally induced? For example, is the crisis
an environmental situation—involving loss of a job, threat of
divorce, fear of violence, or the like? Or, is it an interpersonal,
physical, or emotional problem—like alcohol abuse, infidelity,
fight with a spouse, or the like?

What are the person's resources for coping with the stres-
sors? Here, the helper appeals not to the struggler's dependency
or helpless feelings but to the realistic, growing edges of his
life. Again, what specific goals or plans for action are realistic?
The conversation should draw some plan for managing the
situation into sharp focus. Consultation with or referral to other
individuals, as in Greene's case above, may become part of
the plan.

4. Throughout, one should depend upon God for help.

This is not just a tacked on addendum at the end of the helping process. At all times, God helps persons cope, change, and endure. He provides forgiveness, opportunities to make restitution, and "grace to help in time of need" (Heb. 4:16). His Spirit is the true activator of power, wisdom, decisiveness, and energy. He guides the person in prayer experiences, stimulates initiative, and grants wisdom to follow a wise plan of action. He goes with the individual or family, providing guidance for each step and strength for each act. Without God's help, beyond human skills, we would be lost.

Creative Implications of Crises

Individuals like Wilfred Greene, who are experiencing feelings of being overwhelmed, are highly suggestable. They are grasping at straws, so helpers must be careful not to push for only one solution. Cliff-hangers find it hard to be realistic and practical. They want an end to suffering and an early solution to their pain. Giving advice can be dangerous because it might add another impossible step to one who falters. A person who has messed up his life does not need to add another failure to his list of defeats. Indeed, fear of failing again immobilizes many people so that they appear overly dependent and unable to act.

Crises have a way of becoming creative turning points in human experience. Families that have been deaf to some member's cries for help may be shocked by crisis into new awareness, tenderness, and helpfulness. A congregation's strength can be mobilized by a need. Prayers, calls, and individual acts of attentiveness not only reassure a helpee but they also demonstrate that people really do care. New Testament writers encouraged prayers for the sick, gifts of food and clothing for the poor, visits to prisoners, and tangible expressions of help for hurting persons (Jas. 2:15–16).

Researchers in crisis intervention clinics across the country have discovered that crises may be both helpful and therapeutic.[6] Such boundary situations can become occasions for teachableness and catalysts for change. For example, a man whose back was broken in an automobile accident said: "The only way I could look when my back was broken was up. My family and I were drawn closer to God and to each other as a result of those months of painful recovery." Such an individual may discover new feelings of self-worth and confidence because of time devoted to reflection, prayer, and charting new directions for life. If the helpee is able to cope in crisis times, he senses new strength for life and draws upon inner resources during future difficulties.

The outcome might go the other way, with feelings of bitterness and resentment toward God for permitting some tragedy to happen. All of one's waking moments could revolve around feelings of rejection by heaven, with a desire for revenge, to even life's score. Such an embittered sufferer hurts himself, potential helpers, and all persons about him. Life centers upon rage and revenge as negative potentials, with blindness to the creative providence of God.

Evangelical Christians should be alerted to the risks of forcing someone in a grave crisis to "accept Jesus" as Savior. It is easy, when one functions from a position of strength, to "lord it over" a hurting person or family. Decisions of a religious nature, made under stress as a bargain with God, might backfire once the crisis has passed. God certainly uses crises to bring people to faith. Christian helpers must be open to his Spirit's guidance as they point pained people toward God. He remains profoundly free to draw earth's wounded spirits to himself. The decision of faith, to be authentic, should be theirs.

9 Responding to Needs of the Older Person

On the day that I passed the half century mark, my son and daughter-in-love gave me a book entitled *The Sin of Being Fifty*. Author John B. Johnson, a Baptist minister, details the sin of being fifty in one's mind, heart, body parts, and philosophy of life. Johnson confessed that when he was twenty he wanted to save the world. Now, in his fifties, he just wants to save part of his salary.[1] I have tried to live up to his sage advice about sin and am trying to stay young enough to do so.

The topic "Responding to Needs of the Older Person" seems clear enough until we admit that aging is a highly variable process. It is not easy to predict when one is old. In Sinoe County, Liberia, West Africa, a person is old at forty. In India, mandatory retirement age for many persons is fifty-five. Here, in the United States, about 11 percent of the population is over sixty-five years of age. The Census Bureau estimates that by the year 2000 this figure will increase to 40 percent, or well over eighty million people.

Someone has characterized life's advancing decades as the testing teens, teachable twenties, terrific thirties, fiery forties, forceful fifties, serious sixties, sacred seventies, and aching eighties. Where do you fit in that scheme?

People grow old at different chronological ages. Here is a person in his early fifties who acts eighty. Others are youthful at seventy-five. The Honorable Brooks Hays, former Congressman from Arkansas and in his seventies, once addressed a convention that I attended. "Some of my friends here this evening may not recognize me with this full head of hair," he quipped. "What God hath not wrought, I went out and bought."

One of Maurice Chevalier's memorable lines was, "Aging is terrible, but the alternative is worse." Aging may or may not be bad. It depends! It depends upon one's outlook and readiness to be considered "older;" it depends upon one's younger family members' and friends' attitudes toward aging; it depends upon one's health, financial security, and faith in God. A person who is well-functioning and sturdy at seventy can be changed through a single event—like a fall and fractured hip bone—into a dependent, pain-ridden, emotionally disturbed old man or woman.

To Personalize or Generalize?

One of the real temptations in referring to older persons is to generalize, to lump millions of Americans into an impersonal *they,* then write them off as beyond help or usefulness. The one thing that all people have in common is their uncommonness. Yet our great temptation is to stereotype one another across generational lines. For example, in a mixed age group a man about fifty said to a mid-twenties wife, "I see you as a shy little girl." Perhaps his remark was intended to draw her out of her shell. The second time he said it, she replied angrily "I see you as a dirty old man!"

Stereotypes are expensive. They keep individuals in young, middle, and senior adulthood far apart. Such typecasting presses false roles onto people, drains conversations of true communication, and robs potential relationships of their richness. One of the first ways to care across generational lines is to stop labeling and pigeonholing people into neat, forced compartments.

Bernice Neugarten, an American researcher in aging, has completed a study of more than two thousand persons between the ages of seventy and seventy-nine. Her report deplores stereotyping that causes separations and mistrust between the generations. "So long as we believe that old people are poor, isolated, sick and unhappy (or, to the contrary, powerful, rigid and reactionary)," wrote Neugarten, "we find the prospect of old age particularly unattractive. We can then separate ourselves . . . from older persons and relegate them to inferior status."[2]

When *old* becomes a four-letter word the resulting harm is great. We judge other persons by our own standards or subjective feelings about age. We reject older persons and our own future selves with the mentality of ageism.

Intergenerational relations are also hampered by illusions and impressionistic thinking. In America we foster the illusion of ageless immortality through advertising that features the young—seldom the old. Certain cosmetics, clothes, cars, and sex-laden products exploit the illusion of endless youth.

What is a person's real age? What the calendar says, the retirement regulations of his employer, physical health, or what family or community dictate? We speak of someone being old "before his time" or of someone who is "young for her age." How one feels one should live at sixty or seventy—one's subjective age—may influence living as much as one's biological or social age.

Sociologist Neugarten speaks of the "social clock" regulating people's expectations: being "early" for going to college, "late" getting married, "about right" for entering a profession, and so on. She has suggested the term *personal life time* (in contrast to social or historical time). Part of this concept is the fact that people around fifty to fifty-five begin to think of "time left to live." Whereas, before that age they think of "time since birth."

The truth is a person may appear to be several ages at once: what the calendar says, what the community senses, how the family feels, how the body functions, and the individual's personal life time. "You are as old as you feel," goes the cliché, and there's some truth to that. We each have a biological and a subjective (feeling) age. We can appropriately act that age. When we try to live up to illusions or social impressions that "it's about time for this or that," we can become confused, angry, even estranged from our true selves.

The drama of retirement highlights the tension between personalized and generalized responses to the needs of older people. Picture friends, family, and business associates celebrating a man's mandatory retirement with a dinner party. "I don't see what everybody is so happy about," said one such retiree. "This marks the end for me. Why should I be having a good time?" Deep grief rather than gladness was reflected in his wife's tear-filled eyes. Personal support was offered by well-wishers who passed by the head table. Still, Social Security claims, insurance provisions, financial adjustments, and role shifts from worker to unemployed had to be negotiated. There is something finalistic about being terminated from one's work and disengaged from one's routines. Both personal and general responses are indicated in the aging process.

Learning to Give Care

Care of the aged, like the science of gerontology itself, can be learned. And the place to start is with one's attitude.
Need for respect

Elderly persons appreciate being responded to with respect. Human relationships of all ages are rooted in our common humanity. We are created in God's image and Christians are recreated within the likeness of his Son. Just as beauty lies in the eye of the beholder, so one's identity, tastes, and values will cue his responses to older persons.

The first word is appreciation, positive regard, and undiscourageable goodwill for people. The old among us claim respect for themselves. Hear the words of a man facing retirement: "An old man, his race largely run, points toward retirement. But don't any of you get a picture of an old man on a borrowed horse riding toward the sunset. I have lots of things to do so long as health permits." [3] Such a person wants no pity but a chance to move into a new season of life with dignity. Thus helpers need to see not merely dwindling powers and dependency needs but the growing wisdom and skills of older people. They have earned the right to relax if they want to and claim respect as fellow citizens.

On the other hand, older persons are not always lovable, kind, gracious, and easy to care for. Some oldsters are open to expressions of attentiveness or offers of help. Others seem bitter, caustic, and grim about life's cumulative harvest. Some aged persons are hard to love.

Have you ever noticed reactions of older people when made the subjects of photography? It may be a clue to the way they do all of life. Some feign embarrassment. Some become angry. Others want into the picture. Many appear honored and pleased. I recall two old Italian women, beautiful residents of Florence, who became delighted subjects of my request for a picture. To the contrary, a stocky gentleman with a cane in Copenhagen responded to my request for his picture by sticking out his tongue and making an awful face. I visited a crippled woman, confined to a wheelchair, who cursed her conditions in a convalescent center; yet was welcomed by a mid-eighties widow, who was gracious and serene when I talked with her.

Here is the point. Regardless of your aged relative's or friend's situation, do not make an invalid, statistic, or thing of them. It is far better for people to feel respected and free to do as much for themselves as they reasonably can. For an older person to become a psychological invalid is bad both for him and his caretakers.

Subjective-objective split

Any counseling or helping situation involves both subjective feelings and objective facts. Imagine the problems that might arise when one of an elderly, interdependent pair has died. The person left has all kinds of feelings—grief, loneliness, uncertainty about the future, even guilt about contributing to a partner's death. A woman whose husband had been hospitalized with a serious stroke detailed his activities the day he collapsed. "If I had only helped him lift those heavy sacks out of the car *this* might not have happened," she lamented. One who is left may feel devastated.

A son, daughter, or close relative may become so involved subjectively, after someone's death, that a spontaneous proposal to live together is made. For a potential helper to respond soft-heartedly, out of emotions in a given moment, to the subjectively expressed needs of anyone is risky indeed. An older helpee may face a tremendous crisis, feel temporarily overwhelmed, and make unwise decisions at that time. Matters like housing facilities, ages of one's children still at home, preferences of other family members, and potential clashes of personalities must be accounted for.

An objective look at things, in which a potential helper becomes acquainted with as many facts as possible, is imperative. In this instance, for example, a widowed mother—not physically handicapped and potentially resourceful—would be advised to maintain her own home. If specific help is needed, it can be identified and offered. Given the passing of time, widowhood may not prove an insurmountable problem. A woman who has never driven an automobile or signed a check or filed an income tax form can learn such skills. Furthermore, one helping individual or family need not provide care alone. Physicians, attorneys, registered nurses, social workers, tax consultants, legislators, writers, and educators join churches, synagogues, hospitals, social service agencies, senior citizen centers, adult education programs, and other institutions in a network of resources.

A network of resources

The care of an aged parent often falls the lot of one available, willing, or conscientious child. Some services needed by an older person may be easily mastered: well-balanced meals or clean linens daily on a bed. The more dependent a person is—with physical or emotional handicaps—the more help a care-giver needs. Guard rails for the toilet and bathtub for an infirm person to grasp, or guard rails to keep one from falling out of bed, may become essential. A walker to support a person as he moves about the house or yard may help a weak or handicapped person. Medications must be mastered as to time, potential side effects, dosage, cost, and length of use.

Care should be shared not imposed as a burden on one care-giver. If there is a spouse or companion, the stronger partner should perform as much of the physical aid as possible. He needs a sense of usefulness and will age less quickly with this responsibility and feeling of accomplishment. Several younger family members, if possible, should share caretaking tasks.

Some responses to the needs of the older person are individual, others are institutional; some are spontaneous, others are programmed; some are short-term, others are without a foreseeable end.

Here, for example, is a minister whose church sponsors a "Meals on Wheels" program. His pastoral interest, through one-to-one visits with residents of an older neighborhood, led him to think of total care needs: health, diet, housing, recreation, companionship, worship, and so on.[4] The congregation plans to construct a high-rise apartment center for retired persons adjacent to the church properties. Land acquisition, legal aspects of church-state separation, construction design, financial arrangements, and staffing such a complex have required several years of planning and working.

Few churches or synagogues can do everything with older people—like providing housing, religious nurture, medical care, banking, meals, travel, creative crafts, family counseling, shopping assistance, recreation, and social services. Religious leaders pick and choose the services they can provide—in some instances the services not available elsewhere. They rely upon community resources, United Way-sponsored agencies, programs like medicaid and medicare, Social Security, and adult education centers to share the aging individual's search for meaning and usefulness. Thus, personal and family assets are linked to private and public resources to form a network of care services.

"But," you ask, "what is my response to be—crisis intervention, education, rehabilitation, support, or what?" That depends on one's perspective, social situation, and interpretation of needs.

The Range of Human Needs

The following conversation between a minister and a retired teacher couple illustrates the range of human needs. Both Albert and Vera Ginn are eighty years of age. Since losing his vision a year earlier, Albert has learned to type. He possesses an unusual sense of direction and goes into any room of the house without being led by his wife. Vera is healthy and enjoys life to the fullest. The pastor wants them to feel that they are still a part of things, though they are not active at church.

Pastor: Hello, Vera! How are you this beautiful afternoon?

Vera: Well, if it isn't my pastor! I'm feeling spry as a spring chicken! Come on in and we'll go into this living room where Mr. Ginn is taking his afternoon rest. *(They shake hands and make their way, with additional greetings, to the living room.)* Albert, we have company! Would you like to guess who it might be?

Albert: Yes, I believe I would. Could it by any chance be our pastor?

Vera: Yes! You are right. It is Brother Strauss.

Pastor: Mr. Ginn, it's so good to see you! How have you been doing since I saw you last?

Albert: I've been doing as well as could be expected, I suppose, until week before last. I had to go back to the doctor.

Pastor: Oh, you did? I had not heard about it.

Albert: Yes, I got to the place where I just felt like I did not have as much strength as usual.

Vera: Brother Strauss, he just about stopped eating. That was his trouble.

Pastor: Well, was the doctor able to give you some medicine to help you overcome your poor appetite?

Albert: Oh, yes, he took care of that for me. Seems now that I cannot get enough to eat. *(He laughs.)* Also, he told me I was going to have to take more exercise.

Pastor: Knowing you as I do, I imagine that you have worked out a plan to get more exercise. What have you planned?

Albert: The doctor said that I needed to walk about a mile every day. So when I got home I called my brother Paul to come over. He came and I sent him to buy me a hundred feet of rope.

Pastor: You're not going to play jump rope, are you? *(Both laugh.)*

Albert: No, I had Paul to put up two posts one hundred feet apart and stretch the rope between them. Now, all I have to do is to use the rope as a guide by letting it slip through my right hand as I walk.

Pastor: That means that you have to walk that distance fifty-three times a day. Do you walk all fifty-three times at once, or do you walk some in the morning and some in the afternoon?

Albert: I don't have a set rule to follow, but I keep a count of the times I walk that distance until I have walked my mile.

Vera: I'm the bookkeeper, Brother Strauss. He tells me the number of times he walks the rope; but if I make a mistake he knows that very well too.

Pastor: Do you feel like you are gaining more strength now that you are eating better and taking more exercise?

Albert: Yes, I'm beginning to feel like my old self again.

Pastor: Just as you receive physical strength you can also receive spiritual strength day by day. You can meditate on God's Word and talk with him in prayer.

Albert: You are so right, pastor. Vera always reads the Bible to me every day, then both of us pray together. These moments are our happiest times in every respect.

The pastor offered to read a passage from the Bible if they wished. Mr. Ginn suggested the thirteenth chapter of 1 Corinthians as a favorite selection. Prayer followed his read-

ing of Paul's great love chapter. After a few moments of farewell the pastor departed.

The Ginns' needs might be viewed from several perspectives and stated in existential, economic, medical, political, soci-
ological, and religious terms. Limitations of time and space
do not permit full exploration of all those perspectives. Using
the Ginns' needs as an example of the full range of concerns
felt by older persons, we can specify appropriate responses.
Note how wisely they sought to supply their own necessities,
yet how gracious they were when pastoral support was extended.

I shall suggest six basic needs, common to humanity,
which, viewed as an acrostic, spell the word *enrich*. The needs
include: *e*nvironmental well-being and health; *n*ew experience;
*r*espect (sense of worth); *i*nterpersonal relations (with appreci-
ated companions); *c*reativity (need to contribute to live); and
*h*ope. The concept of enrichment of life, at each stage of development, comes from my own faith commitment. The needs
which I shall briefly describe are universally human.

Environmental well-being and health

The later years should be marked ideally by dependable
people and comfortable surroundings. Though he was legally
blind, Albert Ginn possessed an unusual sense of direction.
He was able to negotiate each room in their home without
Vera's assistance. During one visit with his pastor, Albert said
that his secure sense of direction, with the exception of his
relationship to Jesus Christ, was his best friend.

During the middle years an individual experiences maxi-
mum use of energy, ideas, and vitality. One depends upon
his body to see him through. There is depletion of resources,
a need for wise rhythms in diet, work, rest, and health care.
The aged citizen cannot compartmentalize his economic, physical, spiritual, and emotional well-being. Problems in one area
affect other powers. Blindness, for example, increases one's
dependency upon others, restricts one's movements, and envel-
ops one in darkness. Fears of aging, occasions of dysfunction,

and loss of mental and physical powers intensify the need for well-being in the later years.

The late Lewis Sherrill, who wisely blended psychological and biblical wisdom about persons, sensed that character grows toward simplification in maturity. "The basic formula by which one has met life in his earlier years," wrote the Presbyterian professor, "often tends in his later years to stand out with still greater clarity." [5] Well-being is reinforced by simplifying one's status, family relationships, work, physical surroundings, economic possessions, and character formation. The final drama of one's existence might be played upon the limited stage of a retirement village, nursing home, mobile home park, or extended-care facility. The will to live and reality of death, grief, and loss become constant companions.

New experience

Paradoxically, senior adults need both dependable people and stable surroundings and the freedoms which aging provides. Regimens guided the daily course of Albert and Vera Ginns' experiences and governed their perspectives and movements. Habits order and give meaning to our lives. Roles and relationships—well-defined and durably established—bind life beneficially and thrust human growth toward the ultimate frontiers of becoming.

New experiences and relationships answer mankind's quest for meaning, creativity, and continual growth. Constancy walks hand in hand with change in later years, and that requires courage. The late Paul Tillich held that life requires *the courage to be*—"the self-affirmation of being in spite of the fact of nonbeing." [6] Such courage and openness to the future are rooted in a vital relationship with God.

The apostle Paul lived with a vision of the eternal in the midst of life's evil calamities and tough hardships. "We do not lose heart," he wrote to Christian friends. "Though our outer nature is wasting away, our inner nature is being renewed every day" (2 Cor. 4:16). Albert Ginn understood that. He had just about stopped eating when his doctor told him that he needed more exercise. He worked out new rhythms of walking, diet, and rest.

Leopold Bellak, a New York psychiatrist, wrote in *The Best Years of Your Life* that physical drives decrease with age. Appetites for food, sex, work, play, status, and achievement—such strong driving forces in the younger person—are tempered in the later years. Most people who have attained sixty-five can accept their limitations, wrote Bellak, and can "watch the world around them with some detachment and perspective." [7] Food can be savored for its fine nuances and gourmet subtleties, instead of stuffing oneself like an adolescent. Sexual experiences may be enjoyed when feasible—with leisure, diversity, and pleasure in love-making—rather than exploited with the urgency and frequency of youth. Given the gift of good health, senior citizens are freer to create art, pursue hobbies, read books, follow current events, support politics, play music, enjoy games, engage in conversation, travel, worship, and rest than their younger counterparts.

Respect and sense of worth

The enriched life requires environmental well-being, new experience, and respect for self and other persons. Far Eastern cultures historically have practiced ancestor worship, though that is changing. The respect and sense of worth of which I speak is rooted more in creation, companionship with the Creator, and salvation than in cultural practices. America is at the ebb tide of respect for human personality today.

Both Albert and Vera Ginn affirmed that daily Bible reading and prayer were their "happiest times in every respect." Their sense of worth, like the mystic experience of salvation, came through identification with God. When he was old, Anton Boisen, a pioneer explorer of religious experience in relation to psychic illness and health, wrote of man's hold upon religious reality. The God-relationship produces "peace and joy and stability of character that cannot be taken away," said Boisen, "because it rests on that which outward vicissitude and even death cannot destroy." [8] Regardless of one's economic status and state of health, he can be prized as a person of infinite worth. This need is met uniquely through the Christian faith.

Interpersonal relations

Companions are not optional on life's pilgrimage. We need partners, associates, sojourners, colleagues, and true friends along the way. Companionship is what marriage and the family is all about. Following creation, the Lord God said, "It is not good that the man should be alone; I will make him a helper fit for him" (Gen. 2:18). One senses the delicate dependency relationship, woven into the tapestry of eighty years, between Albert and Vera Ginn. Quiet dignity and attentiveness characterized Pastor Strauss' visit, along with goodwill, humor, and praise.

Life is not a territory to be defended; it is a gift to be shared. One's circle of friends becomes a treasured legacy in old age—people with whom one remembers, rejoices, and hopes.

Contribute and maintain creativity

The enriched life gives to as well as receives from others. Regardless of advancing age, people need to maintain creativity, to contribute to life.

Waiting in decay, with idle hands and a lonely heart, for the end of existence on this earth is not a pleasant prospect. This is what eighty-two-year-old Florida Scott-Maxwell meant when she wrote, "It is waiting for death that wears us down, and the distaste for what we may become." [9] Part of what makes old people feel ostracized in the retirement years is that they are no longer considered as full members of the human community. They seldom generate wealth, go, do, spend, give, or achieve recognition.

A one-hundred-year-old Californian celebrated his birthday with a brother and sister—both in their late nineties. The first one hundred years "have been exciting," he reported to a TV interviewer, "but I wouldn't want to go through it again."

The contribution of which I speak is akin to what Erik

Erikson called integrity versus despair and disgust in *Identity and the Life Cycle.* Integrity, he said, is characterized by an acceptance of one's "own and only life cycle and of the people who have become significant to it as something that . . . permitted of no substitutions." [10] One who possesses integrity said Erikson, accepts other men and women who have contributed dignity and love to life. He defends the dignity of his own life and work, yet remains open to varied life-styles of other people. I see a latter-day openness in older persons who are no longer driven to succeed. Accepting their attainments and limitations, they are no longer afraid of the "powers that be." The Ginns represent those people who have come to terms with what life has brought. Their "own and only" life cycles have been accepted as gifts from God. They are like the righteous person described by the psalmist, "The virtuous . . . will flourish in the courts of our God, still bearing fruit in old age, still remaining fresh and green, to proclaim that Yahweh is righteous" (Ps. 92:12–15, *Jerusalem Bible*).[11]

Hope

Responding to the needs of the older person requires sharpness in recognition and management. Most of us are amateurs, not professionals, in sensing their unique problems and growth directions. Environmental well-being, new experiences, respect, interpersonal relations, and creativeness are five such needs. My acrostic of E-N-R-I-C-H is completed by the requisite of hope.

Hope, biblically, is the bridge between faith and love (1 Cor. 13:13). It binds commitment and caring together and points them into the future. Hope searches morning skies for first rays of light. Hope sees beyond the shadows and silhouettes of sundown by penetrating the shape of tomorrow. Hope lays down the day's burden at nightfall, rests securely, rises refreshed, then proceeds with the day's work. It looks ahead. Hope is not wishing "for" so-and-so or "that" such-and-such will happen. People of faith hope in God, in truth, in trusted persons, and in the healing processes of life.

It was the late psychologist Gordon Allport who noted life is fortified by faith to grow toward the ultimate frontiers of becoming. He claimed that religion "fortifies the individual against the inroads of anxiety, doubt, and despair." Even more, it "provides the forward intention that enables (a person) at each stage of his becoming to relate himself meaningfully to the totality of Being." [12] Allport noted all phases of becoming are subject to arrest. We see arrested development in the meanness and smallness of spirit of some older people, in their paranoid suspicions of mistreatment at life's hands, in their delusional systems and scapegoating defense mechanisms, and in their selfish withdrawal into a tight, lonely world. This was not the Ginns' case. Their spirits were humble, yet soaring on wings of faith, love, and hope. While Albert lived in physical darkness, he moved daily toward the light of eternal love. Theirs was the wisdom, humor, vision, and hope of a good old age.

To claim the frontier of ministry to older persons, a church need not opt for the impossible. The place to begin is with organized visits to homebound persons like the Ginns, enlisting senior adults as cohelpers. Begin by befriending your own aging family members. Listen to their conversations; respond to their expressed needs where possible. Ultimately, in fostering care for aging persons one is prizing his own life. Old age is the future's gift to all people who survive.

10 Care in Life's Great Dangers

We have traveled a lengthy journey together as members of a Christian caring community. Initially, we explored aspects of *being* care-givers with a high degree of commitment to Jesus Christ. Chapter 1 asked, Who cares in a brutal, impersonal world of systems design and planning? Chapter 2 suggested how one may gain the freedom to care, despite feelings of ineptness, anxiety, inadequacy, fear, and ignorance. In chapter 3, the demand for timely, gifted ministry challenged our indifference and temptations of withdrawal, smugness, and Pollyanna-like thinking. Chapter 4 specified how churches could attract and train volunteer helpers to make caring connections with persons in need.

The *doing* of ministry has been explored in five specific areas: skill development (availability, involvement, visitation, prayer, correspondence, and referral), friendship, family needs, microcounseling in crises, and responding to needs of older persons. I have suggested that a caring church requires much altruism from each member, organizes through the use of current structures (like Sunday School, mission action, and deacon groups), and supports outreach and discipleship training. Evangelism and ministry are the twin rails upon which the growing church advances; they should never be set in opposition or conflict with each other.

There are so many concerns that might be explored in a book like this: how to contact persons who have visited one's worship services (prospective members); how to disciple and train new members; how to reach inactive church members; ministry to the elderly and homebound, to families experiencing separation or divorce, to folk facing parent-child conflicts, to the hospitalized, dying, and bereaved; ministry to unemployed and retired individuals; how to reach the non-Christian; and how to help the handicapped. In fact, a curriculum guide might be prepared by the pastoral leader for varied ministry groups in a church. Specific skills for helping persons in every conceivable emergency, need, and crisis might be taught on a year-round basis.

The long-range benefits of a mutual ministry between ordained ministers and laypersons are enormous. I noted at the outset that every pastor needs a pastor. One of the most pressing needs of ministers in modern life is for a greater sense of competence, confidence, and worth in what they are doing. Voluntary lay involvement in the life and work of the Christian congregation would confirm and complement the pastor's day-to-day ministry. It would temper expectations. To achieve mutuality there must be continuing efforts at clarification of roles and definition of the privileges and burdens of such a relationship. Laymen will come to recognize the minister as a human being, with limits, like themselves. As "workers together with God" they will provide mutual support in the midst of mutual effort (2 Cor. 6:1).

Now we shall examine care in three of life's great dangers: estrangement from the church, hospitalized illness, and death and bereavement. These tragedies do not exhaust life's great dangers; rather, they illustrate numerous areas requiring skill development and special acts of ministry. Specific suggestions made in these crises demonstrate ways of caring in other life needs.

The Alienated Church Member

Some time ago the Presbyterian Church in the United States of America began serious work in a much neglected area of pastoral care—reclamation of the inactive member. Called "Found and Lost," it was an effort to activate persons who, for whatever reasons, had become estranged from the church. A dropout is a dropout by whatever name. Baptists have discovered that as many as one-half of all new members received by local congregations become inactive. Five of every ten converts, on the average, participate temporarily in church activities. Then, two of them become inactive, two become nonresident, and one former member in ten turns to another faith.

Numerous articles and books have been written on follow-up evangelism and discipleship training. Sermons have been preached about the church member who, like Demas, drifts away from the Christian faith (2 Tim. 4:10). Leaders in denominational departments of evangelism, mission, and ministry are concerned by the growing number of weak church members. One congregation sliced about one thousand names of inactive members from its rolls; another went to great lengths to locate 960 members that had been found, then lost. Blame has been placed on sources as varied as a "lukewarm pulpit" to the "absolute rightness" and rigid life-styles of some Christians as factors in the church's loss of committed members.

Diagnosing AWOL members is not difficult, but managing a redemptive course of action toward them requires effort. Many city dwellers no longer feel forced into church attendance in order to gain community prestige or family approval. The nearest of kin may be eight hundred miles away. The family, whose absentee father travels all week at work, sticks together on weekends. Middle adults, with the kids grown and gone, may have lost some of their motivation for loyalty. They relax in pleasant suburbs or head out to the farm on Sunday to check on the horses and black Angus cattle.

Possible approaches

Since the church is God's family, the group is incomplete without all its members. Since the church is Christ's body, needing all functioning parts or systems, a member outside the body is in jeopardy. Then, one may ask, what shall we do for persons who become estranged from the church? There are several possible approaches.

(1) The church can isolate its inactives, rejecting those who reject the church. I know a pastor who led his church to clean up the membership rolls the hard way—radical surgery. They had a bragging total of about three thousand members (living and dead) but an accounted for membership of about eighteen hundred. With little thought to the serious consequences that might follow, this leader pruned the deadwood from the trunk of membership.

(2) Ministers, like some physicians, are glad to see so-called neurotic members become inactive or transfer allegiance to another church or cause. Here the approach is to insulate the congregation, and especially the staff, from attacks of bitter or problem members. Such shepherds prefer not to leave the ninety-nine in search of one that has become sick at heart, discouraged, or disgruntled over policies.

(3) A third alternative is to surround persons estranged from the church with a small redemptive group of friends. Such a ministry does not view the church merely as an island of order in a chaotic secular sea nor as a holy business demanding success. Rather, compassion carries the church into human relationships and seeks to build bridges of friendship so that communication can be restored.

Preparing for ministry

How shall a visitor prepare to call on an inactive member? When you schedule a visit, remember that you are a representative of Christ and of people who care. Begin positively, "We are calling on church members as we begin a new year (special program, the Lenten season, an outreach emphasis)." Avoid: "We are calling on inactive members" or "We are checking on those who have not tithed the past two years."

Two, visit because you care, not because someone asked you to call. Make a chore of it and you're in trouble. Someone has said, "It takes a conscientious man to tell whether he's tired or lazy." Counseling persons estranged from the church should be rooted faithfully in the goal of establishing "Christ in you [as] the hope of glory" (Col. 1:27).

Again, identify with the alienated member. Listen to his negative feelings, hurt pride, or criticism. He may not know that he is in trouble. Some persons are afraid of being helped in any meaningful way, especially if it means growth, change, and assuming responsibility. They may want help only on their terms, without repentance and renewal.

Thus we should be aware of the dropout's condition. There are various reasons why people drift away from church.

Some persons are estranged from the church by the crisis of intellect. They may be called the estranged intelligentsia or rebels in search of a humanistic faith. I have a friend, for example, who is a scientist. Years ago he was a student for the ministry. The further he pursued biblical criticism and philosophic problems the further removed he became from the lives of people. Teachers failed to answer adequately some of his questions about "life and death" matters. The man tried several churches. Now, he is a Unitarian and basically humanistic in family life, vocation, and world view.

Some persons are estranged from the church by the crisis of immorality and consequent guilt. They feel like black sheep of the family, not mere playboy Christians. Their moral failures may be ingrained, like that of alcoholics, sociopathic liars, sex deviates, delinquents, and criminals. In some instances, the problem may be an oversensitive conscience rather than misbehavior.

The helper will need good judgment to determine whether a condition is sickness or sin (or both). The physician practices diagnosis in order to name his patient's illness. Christian caregivers might ask of one with a drinking problem, for example, Is he acting in a responsible manner, or compulsively, unable to control his behavior? A person experiencing depression may not be acceptable to the helper because of drinking bouts, but he must experience acceptance in order to be reconciled to God and the church.

Some persons are estranged from church by indifference. Like the lotus-eaters in Tennyson's poem, such people are apathetic toward the church. Yet apathy almost invariably has a clinical history. Some people hold grudges over past slights or hurts. A wife whose husband has a criminal record or lingering psychiatric illness may feel too embarrassed to attend church. Families with a history of retarded or epileptic members or of homosexual practices may appear hostile toward the church. Some people are passive by nature; they are "hearers only" in the apostle James's words. Some people are shy, others are untrained; some get overactive at one time, then collapse in fatigue.

Some persons are estranged from the church because it appears irrelevant to their lives in a technological world. Somewhere, they have known Christian people who substituted superficial piousness for faithful work. Such persons think that theology cannot address human conflict or ethical dilemmas. Perhaps they have known ministers who had nothing more to offer in serious life crises than a smiling face and vague goodwill. Such people, lost from Christian service, may have been offended or rejected by some church leader in the past.

There are numerous other reasons for estrangement. Some persons indifferent to the church are preoccupied with their own success, with family concerns (like an aged parent), or with a profession that takes much of their time. Some have fought long bouts with illness and need to be visited. Others, whose talents have been overlooked, have transferred loyalties and invested their lives in secular or civic organizations. Some persons have been taken advantage of by the church; they feel "put upon" or used. Some have had a deep disappointment, like a missionary whose daughter was dismissed by a Baptist college, and have withdrawn in grief.

Risks of reclamation

How do you deal with people whose minds are closed to the church or whose lives are going in a direction that appears different from God's will? First, some things to avoid. Do not assume that every problem has a simple solution. Do not assume that a shallow excuse or explanation is the answer for a person's behavior. It may be a cover-up for moral chaos or volitional impotence. Some people have no stack pole around which to build their lives. Do not assume the role of an absolute authority. Get off your judgment seat. Approach the person as an enabler, fellow Christian, growth facilitator, and friend. Do not form premature judgments and jump to conclusions.

On the other hand, here are some things that one can do to help persons estranged from the church. Be willing to risk your faith with certain people who are inclined, perhaps temporarily, against the church. Pastors and people alike will have to leave their safe surroundings, venture into homes, and surround dropouts with concern and affection. Listen with your eyes, your ears, and your heart. Theodore Reik speaks of "listening with the third ear," which implies reading between the lines of someone's story. Keep the person's relationship to God threaded into the conversation. Obedience to God is life's greatest achievement. Point them to Christ and the power of his Spirit. Care enough to confront. Direct the person or family into an ongoing church group of which they can feel a responsible part. "Y'all come" is not enough.

You cannot afford the luxury of discouragement while reclaiming persons estranged from the church. Avoid ridicule, rejecting tactics, and rudeness. Any strategy that you adopt in dealing with people should be Christian in motivation and in good social taste. No method is 100 percent effective. Do what you can to create a climate of goodwill and abiding faith in God. They are people for whom Christ died. You can pray for them and place them in his hands.

Hospitalized Illness

Sooner or later tragedy of some sort invades our private citadels. My own life has been touched deeply by my father's accidental death, as well as by my own hospitalization for various surgical procedures. Members of your family, like mine, may have faced malignancy, treatment for emotional disorders, heart attack, gunshot wounds, and serious surgical needs. I had a cousin by marriage who lived fourteen years in a portable

respirator by day and an iron lung by night, paralyzed following poliomyelitis. A courageous Christian, he could not move
even one hand to wipe tears from his eyes or to feed himself
one bite of food during those years. Totally dependent, everything that was done in his life was done by someone else.
He could move only his head, yet he never lost heart. His
example of quiet heroism, against the odds, has encouraged
many persons who knew him.

No generalization is going to fit all cases of illness; it is
too personal for that. Hospitalization is not merely an interrup-
tion of life; it is life at a growing edge. A helper will not
know the inner world of a patient unless he shares his feelings.
Neither should a visitor pry into a person's private emotions
because the individual spirit is holy ground. A sickroom is
sacred territory. Frequent visits will reveal a variety of moods
and needs as the person depends upon a team of healers to
see him through a hospitalization experience.

Whether you enter a hospital as a patient or as a visitor,
you will increase your effectiveness by considering certain
facts. One, while accidents and illnesses are common occur-
rences from the hospital's perspective, they are not customary
for your neighbors. Hospitalized illnesses and surgical procedures disrupt life's serenity and threaten the security of persons
and their families. Causes of illness or injury vary: industrial
accident, poisoning, drug overdose, accidental burn or fall, infection of a vital organ, and invasion by disease. "If it's *my*
toe that's being cut on," someone quipped," then it's *major*
surgery." For most folk going to the hospital provokes a crisis.
Life's customary anxieties are intensified.

The nature of one's condition, in the second place, determines his attitudes toward hospitalization and needs as a patient. An executive's annual checkup in the medical center is
a preventive measure, involving temporary dislocation from
work, but it is not a threatening trip. An aged father being
placed permanently in a convalescent home against his will
provokes a unique set of responses in him and his children.

Removal of a child's tonsils has become a simple procedure, requiring overnight hospitalization. Open-heart surgery on the family breadwinner, on the other hand, is another matter.

You do not have to know the exact nature or details of a patient's condition in order to visit effectively. Simply remember, when calling, that *acute* illnesses usually involve short-term hospitalization, and the *chronic* conditions may persist even when a patient returns home.

Three, the patient's capacity for coping with the upset, accident, or surgical procedure will determine the degree of crisis he experiences. Some people imagine the worst; they fear cancer or, in case of anxiety, fear they are going crazy. Your own relationships with the patient and family will determine how effective and useful you can be during the illness.

As you visit a patient or family member, you can determine his maturity and spiritual resources for facing the situation. You will see patients deny death, hoping that God or the doctor will work a miracle. Others will be hostile, asking, "Why did God permit this to happen?" To such a soul-searching question you might reply, "Tell me what you think." Dependency needs will be evidenced. "We just don't know how to appreciate good health," someone might say. Another will confess, "If it weren't for God and my good neighbors, I don't know what I'd do."

Guilt can be detected in some families. "God let Charlie fall because . . . ," they rationalize, trying to connect a single sin with a specific accident. Such logic is unwise because the innocent suffer along with the guilty. All sin brings suffering, but all suffering is not the result of sin. You or I may suffer, not because of our sin but because of someone else's fault— as in an automobile accident. It is encouraging to work with families facing illness who say: "Joe is sick. With God's help he can be well."

When you enter the halls of a modern hospital remember that the combined efforts of the entire medical and nursing staffs are aimed at restoring health, prolonging life. You represent God and a specific church—redemptive group—in the midst of a healing environment. Thus you will wish to be a wholesome guest in a person's room, as well as an effective spiritual instrument during the visit.

Visit the sick not as a pious habit or good deed for the day but with the intent of supporting the patient or family in the lonely hospital setting. (*Support* is not to be confused with reciting jokes, sharing gossip, or divulging morbid details of a mutual friend's dying condition.) Do not visit when you are sick.

All of us have visited enough to recognize that *we are not indispensable to the patient's recovery.* In protecting the patient's welfare, hospital visitors will be guided by the following principles.[1]

1. Respect the hospital's policy about time for visitation. Schedules are enforced in obstetrics and nursery departments to protect the welfare of women after labor and childbirth and to reduce infection among infants.

2. Secure information about patients prior to entering a room. Correct room assignments are provided through an information service. If a door is closed, knock before entering. A nurse or aide may assist you with information about the person or in gaining admission to the room.

3. Heed signs on the door, such as *Isolation, X-ray, No Visitors,* and the call light. They are placed at the room's entrance to protect the patient, to prolong his life, and to inform personnel if the patient has been taken to another department.

4. Introduce yourself as you are received into the sickroom. Some patients under the influence of drugs or sedatives may be woozy or asleep. Aged patients or accident victims may not recall your name or even recognize you. Since this is his room and the host is sick, be at your best. Let the patient take the lead in shaking hands.

5. Remember that patients are sometimes unduly sensitive because of pain, uncertainty, infection, and so on. Do not say

anything knowingly that will linger in the patient's mind and worry him after your departure. If the patient appears asleep or unconscious or does not respond, his hearing faculties may still be at work. It is best to visit with family members outside the room in cases of critical illness.

6. Just because you are up and the patient is down, don't assume a patronizing air toward the sick person. You may be next! Be genuine in your interest and concern. Seek to represent God faithfully in that particular patient's case. For example, avoid clichés or stock comments.

7. Stand or sit in the patient's line of vision. Be friendly to others in the room but, where possible, concentrate on a face-to-face ministry with the patient. Avoid leaning on the bed or jarring equipment like an infusion flask or an oxygen tent.

8. Give the patient time to respond to you. Listen to feelings, as well as words, being expressed and respond on the feeling level. If a person is anxious, for example, say, "It's really hard not knowing what is wrong" (or the like), so he senses that you care.

9. The frequency and length of your hospital visits will be determined by varied factors: the distance of your residence from the hospital, relationship to the patient, his or her capacity to receive company, and so on. No one can tell you how long a visit should be. Its duration will vary according to the patient's condition and responsiveness, interruptions, and presence of other visitors.

10. Ordinarily you will excuse yourself when the patient's meal is brought or when the doctor or nurse indicates a need for examination or treatment.

You may desire to leave a card or gift as a token of your affection for the patient. When our son was a second grader, years ago, his teacher visited him during a period of hospitalization. She brought picture greetings from his fellow pupils in elementary school and an ivy plant in a dog-shaped container. He was too weak from fever and infection to say much at the time, but he cherished those tokens of friendship and love in days of recovery.

Normally the antennae of a person's soul are extremely sensitive to signals from God and his servants during illness. You will not have to carry God into a sickroom. He is already present in the midst of the treatment situation. If you wish to read the Scriptures or voice a prayer, don't use such resources as a means to escape from the room. These are not contrivances for avoiding uncomfortable relationships. They are "at home" in any relationship which recognizes God in the midst (Matt. 18:20) and seeks to honor his name. In a sense, the entire visit should be conducted in the spirit of prayer, recalling that "from the most high comes healing."

Death and Bereavement

I called upon a cancer patient whom the physicians had pronounced terminally ill. She talked of getting stronger and returning to her junior high school teaching activities. "What if it should go the other way, Mary Ann?" I inquired, deliberately giving that lovely woman an opportunity to talk about her death—if she desired. "Oh, it won't," she denied, refusing to speak of life's end. The desire to avoid references to death led her to talk about little things that gave meaning to each day.

Biblical man viewed biological death as a dreadful certainty resulting from sin and looked uncertainly to life beyond death. Second Samuel 14:14 records a dialogue between a king and a woman of Tekoa, "We must all die; we are like water spilt on the ground, which cannot be gathered up again." The ancient preacher mused, "The living know that they will die" (Eccl. 9:5); and the psalmist anticipated, "The years of our life are threescore and ten" (Ps. 90:10). Allusions to death are like mist upon the mountains in the Wisdom Literature. Life is "like grass . . . a flower . . . the wind . . . like a river wasting away."

Resolute hope appears in New Testament writings where death is swallowed up in the victory of eternal life. This apostolic hope was based upon Christ's teachings and his acknowledged resurrection from the grave.

Man's attitudes toward death are determined largely by his sociohistorical background and religious beliefs. In humanistic thought death is the end of all existence. Such materialistic conclusions are certified by dissolution of the body's cellular and chemical components at death. Victorian man's anxious longings for immortality appear in the works of Browning and Tennyson. Romantic poets like Byron and Shelley courted death. Modern Americans are in the process of making up their minds about the mystery of death.

When Abraham Lincoln lived, the average life expectancy was forty-five to fifty. Now, it is seventy to seventy-five in the United States, with promise of a greatly extended life span. Americans seeking immortality are told to "think young." Still the living know that they will die.[2] Death is no stranger. Rather it is our constant companion. Death never takes a holiday.

Death is often in the thoughts of church members, yet seldom in their conversations. The subject can be suppressed, yet it invades one's dreams as a phantom from a far-off planet. Whatever one says of death will be both right and wrong. It will not be the voice of experience. Much data is not merely unknown but unknowable.

We do not know, for example, when a person is supposed to die. Doctors attending a female patient in her late twenties told her parents that, according to her longevity curve and condition, she should be dead. But she defied every estimated deadline they set. Their explanation? "She is young and has a great will to live."

Swiss-born psychiatrist Elisabeth Kübler-Ross traced the feelings of dying persons through five definable stages following interviews with four hundred patients in Chicago hospitals.[3] The stages include: (1) *denial*—"No, not me"; (2) *anger*—"Why me?"; (3) *bargaining*—"Yes, me, but if I do so-and-so will I live?"; (4) *depression*—"Yes, me . . . but oh no"; and (5) *acceptance*—"Yes, into thy hands . . . . " She has been at the forefront of the death-awareness movement in America and believes in a life after life based on her observations and experiences.

We do not know when a person gives up hope. For example, we are not sure how much of a suicide's self-system has been destroyed before physical death occurs. Psychologist James Hillman theorizes that, in philosophic thought, *"all death is suicide,* and the choice of method is only more or less evident, whether car-crash, heart-attack, or those acts usually called suicide." [4] You and I would observe, to the contrary, that many deaths are accidental, others result from disease, and that infants' deaths are not suicidal.

On the other hand, the suicidal person may not be aware that he is killing himself. A chaplain of a state psychiatric hospital told some friends of having been ticketed three times for excessive speeding. "I may want to leave that place more than I'll admit," he said jestingly.

Some persons drive themselves mercilessly without honestly recognizing that death is their goal. Others are impatient with this life. They demand a fuller life, freedom from this world, by choosing how and when they shall die. Suicide becomes a way of escape for twenty thousand or more Americans each year. In addition to the successful suicides, there are several times that number of attempted suicides. Some cities, like Los Angeles, have established Suicide Prevention Centers in an attempt to cope with this problem.

The moment a child is born he is old enough to die—an Rh factor gone awry, suffocation or strangulation, congenital malformation, or birth trauma. For some persons dying is drawn out over months of waiting—cancer, heart disease, stroke. Perhaps there is time to put one's house in order. Yet, in much of modern dying, there is no conscious moment of death. Rather, there may be prolonged coma or life is snuffed out instantly. This is true of mass bombings in war, victims of criminal attack, a flaming automobile wreck, the victims of a plane crash, or a ship's sinking into a watery grave.

Trying to cope with death raises perplexing questions. Scientists have confirmed the biblical assertion that we are always dying and being renewed (2 Cor. 4:16). While physicians soften our dreadful anticipation of dying by placing terminally ill persons in medical settings, out of sight; while frozen interment promises limited immortality; while mourning has been modified by sedation and the grief process interpreted by psychiatrists, man cannot forever repress his questions.[5] One can take his mind off things just so long.

Ministers presiding at memorial services for man's final "rite of passage" know that they are skirting the edges of a great mystery. For the survivors, who shrink from the dark abyss, death in imagination is a reality. Anxieties about death must be faced by the church. No matter how we seek to outwit it with substitute forms of immortality (art, sex, influence) death will not be denied its harvest.

People who care cope with a multitude of responses from the dying and members of the family.

1. Some persons deny death's reality.

They are in love with life. For example, a youth of twenty, recently married and a senior in college, was fatally injured in an automobile accident. What were Richard's last words before lapsing into a coma? "Don't cheat me, God," his family and intimate friends heard him pray, "I want to live." Soon his room was filled with stillness. Life faded like a vapor in the morning sun.

To escape death we find a scapegoat, like the funeral directors in Jessica Mitford's *The American Way of Death.* A movie *The Loved One* turns death into a joke. And the plot of playwright Ionesco's *How to Get Rid of It* concerns a corpse that grows and grows until it floats away like a giant balloon.

2. The living generally do not want to burden their family and friends.

Some men prepare elaborately through legal advice for estate settlement. Even the poor hope to be buried decently.

If you listen to the whispered words between friends in a convalescent center, there is a desire to avoid suffering. "I hope that God takes me quickly," admits one. "I don't want to burden my family." The friend agrees, "Yes, I hope that I don't suffer like so-and-so."

3. In a world of gigantic death we find many people hardened to the subject.

They bring to death what they bring to life—a materialistic outlook. This is true in war-torn lands. In America, the child who watches TV Westerns, gangster, and war films becomes toughened to death's tragic dimensions. He never sees anyone really die or an animal—unless a pet is injured fatally by a car. Imagine his response to the news that grandfather is dead. "Who shot him?" he might ask in Matt Dillon fashion.

4. Some people insist the power of life and death remains in their hands.

This is true of any physician who has practiced any form of mercy-killing, including withdrawal of life-extending drugs or equipment from terminally ill patients. The suicide, as we have said, may view his exit from earth as an act of courage— thoughtfulness for his family or mercy for himself. Violent men, whether criminals or temporarily insane, treat life indifferently. Before he died, ex-marine Charles Whitman killed fifteen persons—including his wife and mother—and wounded thirty-one more from his sniper's post at the University of Texas.

5. Perhaps you have known persons who faced death with courage mixed with dread and misgivings.

Such was the case of a Christian minister who knew that he was dying. "I know that the time is short, Dr. Kline," said the fifty-year-old minister whom we shall call George. "I do not want to prolong my life with humane drugs and modern gadgets."

The two agreed that the patient would remain at work and at home with his family as long as possible. One Friday, a friend stopped by his office. "How is it going, George?" he inquired. "I can't complain," replied the dying man, who refused to give in to pain and depressive feelings. Within a week he was gone. A humanistic observer might call that stoicism. To me it appears to have been courageous Christian realism.

The experience raises the question of whether to tell a person that death is near. Members of the health team do not agree on this ethical question. I believe sick persons have a right to know the truth to the limit of their ability to bear it. I have talked with a score or more physicians about this matter. With few exceptions, they let each patient know the truth and assist him to live as fully as possible with the truth. Yet doctors can be wrong. Cause and effect laws do not operate identically in all people. Resistance to illness differs with each patient. Thus it is best to face critical illnesses with skilled medical attention and realistic Christian assurance.

The hospice approach to care of the terminally ill is growing in America. The hospice is a place for care of the dying. This concept holds that the most important needs of the dying are relief from pain and closer contact with loved ones. Hospice societies have been organized in many states, and there is a trend to permit the dying to end their lives in peace and dignity, possibly at home, with appropriate help and services.

There are grief experiences in life more oppressive than death: divorce, delinquency, infidelity, invalidism, or mental illness, for example. Comforters of those who mourn should understand that the process of grief works so that its developmental stages may be met with appropriate resources.[6] Normal expressions of grief—shock, protests, tears, stereotyped thinking, anxious dependence, and impulsive talking about the deceased—permit a healthy cleansing of emotions. The widow who sits tearlessly through a funeral service, unable to express her true feelings, may find herself deeply depressed in future weeks.

Grief's wound has been called "the illness that heals itself." Under appropriate conditions of support within a community of love, the bereaved person is free to work through his or her loss. Bereavement properly becomes *grief work* when a person, rather than avoiding reality, (1) accepts his loss and the suffering that goes with it, (2) consolidates memories of the past with future plans, and (3) assumes responsibility for life's new demands. Thus, repressive words, including the misuse of the Scriptures, should be avoided. When a person's heart is broken he doesn't need explanations but friends who will stand by, plus the healing presence of God. When grief has its work, through the resources of the Christian funeral and aftercare, life must go on.

Conclusion

The Christian faith faces numerous challenges today: organized evil and social injustice, lawlessness and inhumanity, indifference within and opposition without. Critics of the church argue that life's real issues should be met by social planners, economists, politicians, and militarists, not by ministers or laymen.

This book has dared us to admit that a Christian's role as a public citizen cannot be separated from his private life. The new and future minister or layman will not merely argue for the Ten Commandments and New Testament faith. People who care will act upon their convictions and involve themselves in human needs—private and public. Their goal is that the *helped* become *helpers*. In a climate of love they advance the kingdom of God.

Notes

Chapter 1

1. From the King James Version of the Bible, hereafter cited as KJV.

2. See the following books for an introduction to social systems theory: W. Robert Beavers, *Psychotherapy and Growth: A Family Systems Perspective* (New York: Bruner/Mazel, 1977); Frederick K. Berrien, *General and Social Systems* (New Brunswick, N. J.: Rutgers University Press, 1968); Gerald Caplan, *Support Systems and Community Mental Health* (New York: Behavioral Publications, 1974); Kenneth de Greene, *Systems Psychology* (New York: McGraw Hill, 1970).

3. The substance of this section appeared in C. W. Brister, *People Who Care* (Nashville: Broadman Press, 1967), pp. 23–28.

Chapter 2

1. Annie Dillard, *Pilgrim at Tinker Creek* (New York: Harper's Magazine Press, 1977), p. 2.

2. Walter Starcke, *The Ultimate Revolution* (New York: Harper and Row, 1969), p. 33.

3. See Alan Keith-Lucas, *This Difficult Business of Helping* (Richmond: CLC Press, 1965), pp. 6–13.

4. See David L. McKenna, *The Jesus Model* (Waco: Word Books, 1977).

Chapter 3

1. William A. Holmes, *Tomorrow's Church: A Cosmopolitan Community* (Nashville: Abingdon Press, 1968), pp. 50–51.

2. Gibson Winter, *The New Creation as Metropolis* (New York: The Macmillan Co., 1963), pp. 136–141.

3. Adapted from Paul Tournier, *A Place for You* (New York: Harper and Row, 1968).

4. John Steinbeck, *Travels with Charley* (New York: Franklin Watts, Inc., 1962), p. 10.

5. Jürgen Moltmann, *Religion, Revolution, and the Future,* trans. M. Douglas Meeks (New York: Charles Scribner's Sons, 1969), p. xv.

6. William E. Hulme, *Two Ways of Caring* (Minneapolis: Augsburg Publishing House, 1973), pp. 96–97.

7. Paul Tillich, *Love, Power, and Justice* (New York: Oxford University Press, 1954), pp. 11–12.

Chapter 4

1. Cited by Gene E. Bartlett, "Preaching in Suburbia," *Andover Newton Quarterly* (March, 1971), p. 192.

2. From *The New English Bible.* Copyright © The Delegates of the Oxford University Press and the Syndics of the Cambridge University Press, 1961, 1970. Reprinted by permission. Subsequent quotations are marked NEB.

3. An unpublished address by O. T. Binkley, president emeritus, Southeastern Baptist Theological Seminary, stimulated my ideas about Christian response to humanity's hurt.

4. Jeffrey K. Hadden, "Some Prerequisites for Lay Involvement," *Pastoral Psychology* (June, 1971), p. 10.

5. Anne K. Stenzel and Helen M. Feeney, *Volunteer Training and Development* (New York: The Seabury Press, 1968), pp. 85–87.

Chapter 5

1. Carlyle Marney, *Priests to Each Other* (Valley Forge: Judson Press, 1974), pp. 11–14.

2. Further resources in counseling may be found in C. W. Brister, *The Promise of Counseling* (San Francisco: Harper and Row, 1978); Gary Collins, *How to Be a People Helper* (Santa Ana, Ca.: Vision House Publishers, 1976); and Alan Keith-Lucas, *Giving and Taking Help* (Chapel Hill: The University of North Carolina Press, 1972).

Chapter 6

1. Books which help parents to understand children include C. W. Brister, *It's Tough Growing Up* (Nashville: Broadman Press, 1971); James Dobson, *Hide or Seek* (Old Tappan, N. J.: Fleming H. Revell Co., 1974); and J. Roswell Gallagher and Herbert I. Harris, *Emotional Problems of Adolescents,* 3d ed. (New York: Oxford University Press, 1976).

2. C. S. Lewis, *The Four Loves* (New York: Harcourt, Brace, Jovanovich, Inc., 1960), pp. 80–90.

3. Grady Nutt, *Agaperos* (Nashville: Broadman Press, 1977), p. 138–139.

4. The splendid essay by Morton M. Hunt, "The Decline and Fall of Friendship," *Saturday Evening Post* (Sept. 15, 1962), pp. 64–66 has influenced my thought about friendship.

5. The single life requires its own unique disciplines. See Gary R. Collins, ed. *It's OK to Be Single* (Waco: Word Books, 1976); Margaret Evening, *Who Walk Alone: A Consideration of the Single Life* (Downers Grove, Ill.: InterVarsity Press, 1974; and Britton Wood, *Single Adults Want to Be the Church, Too* (Nashville; Broadman Press, 1977).

Chapter 7

1. Myron C. and Mary Ben Madden, *The Time of Your Life* (Nashville: Broadman Press, 1977), pp. 85–97.

2. Lewis J. Sherrill, *The Struggle of the Soul* (New York: The Macmillan Co., 1952); Alex Haley, *Roots* (New York: Doubleday and Company, Inc., 1976); Gail Sheehy, *Passages: Predictable Crises of Adult Life* (New York: E. P. Dutton and Co., 1976).

3. John R. Claypool, *Stages:The Art of Living the Expected* (Waco: Word Books, 1977).

4. See Terry Berger, *How Does It Feel When Your Parents Get Divorced?* (New York: Julian Messner, 1977); Roger H. Crook, *An Open Book to the Christian Divorcee* (Nashville: Broadman Press, 1974); Lofton Hudson, *'Til Divorce Do Us Part* (New York: Thomas Nelson, Inc. 1973).

5. John N. and Nellie Carver, *The Family of the Retarded Child* (New York: Syracuse University Press, 1972); Harold Stubblefield, *The Church's Ministry in Mental Retardation* (Nashville: Broadman Press, 1965).

6. T. B. Maston, *God Speaks Through Suffering* (Waco: Word Books, 1977).

7. See Wayne E. Oates, *When Religion Gets Sick* (Philadelphia: Westminster Press, 1970); and Myron Madden, *Raise the Dead!* (Waco: Word Books, 1975).

Chapter 8

1. Gene W. Brockopp, "Crisis Intervention Theory, Process and Practice," D. Lester and Gene W. Brockopp, *Crisis Intervention and Counseling by Telephone* (Springfield, Ill.: Charles C. Thomas, 1973), pp. 89–104; see Donna C. Aguilera and Janice M. Messick, *Crisis Intervention: Theory and Methodology,* 2d ed. (St. Louis: C. V. Mosby Co., 1974); Robert R. Carkhuff, *The Art of Problem Solving* (Amherst, Mass.: Human Resource Development Press, 1973); and Howard W. Stone, *Crisis Counseling* (Philadelphia: Fortress Press, 1976).

2. See Howard J. Clinebell, *Basic Types of Pastoral Counseling* (Nashville: Abingdon Press, 1966), pp. 163–164.

3. Eudora Welty, *The Optimist's Daughter* (New York: Random House, 1972), pp. 99, 131.

4. David K. Switzer, *The Minister as Crisis Counselor* (Nashville: Abingdon Press, 1974), p. 54.

5. Warren L. Jones, "The A-B-C Method of Crisis Management," *Mental Hygiene* (January, 1968), pp. 87–89.

6. Brockopp, "Crisis Intervention Theory, Process and Practice," p. 94.

Chapter 9

1. John B. Johnson, *The Sin of Being Fifty* (Grand Rapids, Mi.: Baker Book House, 1964), p. 10.

2. Bernice Neugarten, "Grow Old Along with Me! The Best Is Yet to Be," *Psychology Today* (Dec. 1971), pp. 45–48, 79–81. See Jean Abernethy, *Old Is Not a Four-Letter Word!* (Nashville: Abingdon Press, 1975).

3. John J. Hurt, *The Baptist Standard* (Oct. 20, 1976), p. 7.

4. See proposals by Robert W. McClellan, *Claiming a Frontier: Ministry and Older People* (Los Angeles: University of Southern California Press, 1977).

5. Lewis Joseph Sherrill, *The Struggle of the Soul* (New York: The Macmillan Co., 1952), p. 140.

6. Paul Tillich, *The Courage to Be* (New Haven: Yale University Press, 1952), p. 155.

7. Leopold Bellak, *The Best Years of Your Life* (New York: Atheneum, 1975), p. 11.

8. Anton T. Boisen, *The Exploration of the Inner World* (New York: Harper Torchbooks, 1962), p. 293.

9. Florida Scott-Maxwell, *The Measure of My Days* (New York: Alfred A. Knopf, 1968), p. 138.

10. Erik H. Erikson, *Identity and the Life Cycle, Psychological Issues,* vol. 1 (New York: International Universities Press, Inc., 1959), p. 98.

11. *The Jerusalem Bible,* (Dorton, Lougman and Todd, Ltd. and Doubleday and Co., Inc., 1966), p. 877.

12. Gordon W. Allport, *Becoming* (New Haven: Yale University Press, 1955), p. 96.

Chapter 10

1. For additional guidance see William G. Justice, *A Handbook for Visiting the Sick: Don't Sit On the Bed!* (Nashville: Broadman Press, 1973).

2. See "Living with Dying," *Newsweek* (May 1, 1978), pp. 52–63.

3. Elisabeth Kübler-Ross, *On Death and Dying* (New York: The Macmillan Co., 1969).

4. James Hillman, *Suicide and the Soul* (New York: Harper and Row, 1964), p. 62.

5. See Erich Lindemann, "Symptomatology and Management of Acute Grief," *American Journal of Psychiatry,* 101 (1944), pp. 144–148.

6. See Brister, *Pastoral Care in the Church* (New York: Harper and Row, 1977), pp. 249–255; John Claypool, *Tracks of a Fellow Struggler* (Waco: Word Books, 1974); and Wayne E. Oates, *Pastoral Care and Counseling in Grief and Separation* (Philadelphia: Fortress Press, 1976).